Folding Paper Cranes

"With a lovely combination of prose and poetry, Leonard Bird bears witness to the terrible crimes committed by the United States government against innocent citizens in the name of 'national security.' Bird gives us a deeply personal view… always with beautiful writing and with a generosity of spirit that lifts the reader's heart."

—Leslie Marmon Silko, author of
Almanac of the Dead and *Ceremony*

"Bird's deeply moving and compelling memoir takes an important place in a body of work bearing witness to the terrible reality of nuclear testing and the use of nuclear weapons."

—Mary Dickson, author of the essays "Downwinders All" and "Living and Dying with Fallout"

"Bird's story is sobering and triumphant, heroic and healing. His is the sane entreaty to the powers-that-be to reconsider the effects of using and testing nuclear weapons. *Folding Paper Cranes* is perhaps one of the most important books to come out in decades, a wake-up call for all of us."

—Pamela Uschuk, director of the
Salem College Center for Women Writers

"To survive not only cancer but despair, the author must learn from Japan's *Hibakusha* (survivors of the blasts over Hiroshima and Nagasaki) how to reorient in the world—what to believe and how. This book is rich with its author's spiritual earnings, a wealth we may share."

—William Pitt Root, author of *Trace Elements from a Recurring Kingdom*

"To read this work is to follow closely one man's journey to come to terms with devastating experiences—and to participate with him as he learns, finally, to place his hopes for the future in the hands of the next generation of children."

—Karen M. Moloney, Weber State University

folding
paper cranes

an **atomic** memoir

by Leonard Bird

THE UNIVERSITY OF UTAH PRESS
Salt Lake City

09 08 07 06 05   5 4 3 2

 The Defiance House Man colophon is a registered trademark of
The University of Utah Press. It is based upon a four-foot-tall,
ancient Puebloan pictograph (late PIII) near Glen Canyon, Utah.

LIBRARY OF CONGRESS CATALOGING-IN-PUBLICATION DATA
Bird, Leonard.
  Folding paper cranes : an atomic memoir / by Leonard Bird.
    p. cm.
  Includes bibliographical references.
  ISBN 0-87480-824-3 (pbk. : alk. paper)
  1. Bird, Leonard. 2. United States. Marines—Biography. 3. Nuclear
weapons—Testing—Nevada. 4. Cancer—Patients—United States—
Biography. 5. Atomic bomb victims—United States—Biography. 6.
Atomic bomb—Health aspects. I. Title.
  VE25.B57A3 2005
  355.02'17—dc22   2005000304

Cover images: Shot Hood. U.S. Department of Energy photograph; *Hands Holding
Origami Crane,* Tadashi Miwa/Dex Image/Getty Images

"The Mourning Dove" first appeared in *Connections...2,* summer 1976, and later
in Leonard Bird, *River of Lost Souls* (Guadalupita, NM: Tooth of Time, 1977).

An abbreviated version of "Life in the Dead Zone" appeared
in the *Durango Herald (Colorado),* December 5, 1994.

For
SHIGEMITSU OGURA
NOVEMBER 12, 1922–NOVEMBER 11, 1990

Who dreamed of greater human understanding,
and who founded the International Education System;
and for his son Tsuyoshi, who carried on the dream;
and for Tsuyoshi's old friend Ray Hagiwara,
whose first words to me were,
"I have a passion for world peace."

Contents

Acknowledgments

Over the long years it has taken to complete this thin witness, I have received help and encouragement from family, friends, and my colleagues at Fort Lewis College, where I taught from 1969 until 2000. A number of folks have been particularly helpful. I would like to thank my friend and colleague Jim Ash for introducing me to the Oguras and making possible my two returns to Hiroshima; Fort Lewis College for the sabbatical that allowed me time to write the first draft; the poets Renee Gregorio and John Brandi for their careful reading of that draft and their suggestions for expanding and pulling the work together; my old colleagues, Mark Coburn—for stylistic and organizational suggestions, and Kathryn Moller, who turned lines from this book into a theatrical production; and my wife, Jane Leonard, who critiqued several drafts, provided unstinting moral support, and penned the lovely monoprints that accompany this work.

Preface

This collage of poems and stories constitutes a memoir of sorts, and attempts to integrate the detritus of four encounters with nuclear war: three journeys to Hiroshima (1954, 1981, and 1993) and one forced visit as a young Marine to the irradiated trenches of Yucca Flat. Though the encounters differ, collectively they move through a slough of angst and despair to a positive vision. By the end of the fifth narrative, "A Flight of Cranes," the collection has become a prayer of hope, not for ourselves so much as for our children.

Hiroshima is, of course, best known for its having been all but totally destroyed when, in an attempt to push Japan toward immediate and unconditional surrender, America uncorked the nuclear genie nineteen hundred feet over the precise center of town and killed almost a hundred thousand people, mostly civilians. Yucca Flat, less infamous by far, is a barren plain that comprises Area 9a of the Nevada Test Site (NTS). At the NTS between 1951 and 1962 the Atomic Energy Commission triggered 101 atmospheric detonations, many of which provided an open-air laboratory for calculating the short-term effects of atomic bombs on American combat troops. The only short-term effect being gauged was "Will they or will they not panic?" The Atomic Energy Commission and the Department of Defense proved to be far less concerned with any possible long-term effects on the troops. The atmospheric detonations began in 1951 in reaction to the Soviet Union's emerging nuclear capability and ended in 1962 in reluctant response to increasing public opposition. Presumably safe, but notoriously dirty, underground detonations continued for another thirty years until President George H. W. Bush signed the Comprehensive Nuclear Test Ban Treaty, which President George W. Bush is in the process of abandoning.

The most significant series of tests, the sixth, was Operation Plumbbob, which took place between April and October of 1957. The year is notable not only for the unprecedented amount of radioactive kilotonnage the series produced but also for its marking an important turning point in history: By the end of the year, America possessed a stockpile of 6,744 nuclear weapons, while the Soviet Union had only 660. For the first time in history, our species had in hand sufficient tools to destroy itself.

Operation Plumbbob produced twenty atmospheric detonations and one frightening misfire and spewed into the atmosphere 58,300 kilocuries of radioactive iodine (I-131), more than twice the amount contributed by any other blast series. Iodine-131 makes up less than 2 percent of the irradiated isotopes in fallout, and it is far from the most dangerous. Nevertheless, thus far I-131 is the *only* isotope to have been studied in depth by the National Cancer Institute, and then only as it relates to thyroid cancer. The National Cancer Institute estimates that the radioactive iodine from Plumbbob alone will cause at least thirty-five thousand additional cases of thyroid cancer, and that those additional cases will in turn lead to twenty-seven hundred additional deaths.[1] Iodine-131 has a half-life of about eight minutes. Strontium-90, which causes bone and blood cancer, has a half-life of about eight thousand years. Because I-131 represents just 2 percent of fallout, the data should strongly motivate us to extrapolate. The government, that is to say the Atomic Energy Commission and the Department of Defense, both denied knowledge, responsibility, and even the possibility of deleterious consequences. As far as they were concerned, the fallout posed no danger.[2]

The most devastating bomb in the Plumbbob series was Shot Hood, a two-stage, thermonuclear device with a yield of seventy-four kilotons, by far the largest, dirtiest, and most controversial device ever exploded over North America.[3] From ground zero in Hiroshima, the zone of total destruction extended two kilometers in all directions. Shot Hood was roughly six times greater than Little Boy, the bomb that America detonated over Hiroshima.

In some ways Shot Hood has proved to be my nemesis. In other ways, however, Hood has also been my salvation. In 1954, as an eighteen-year-old Marine stationed on the north slope of Mt. Fuji, I reluctantly accompanied two of my buddies to Hiroshima and its two-year-old International Park for World Peace. From that visit I gleaned little but awed confusion. I could not grasp why the *Hibakusha* (best translated as "atomic-bomb survivors") had poured so much of their scant resources and despairing energy into a "peace" park, even before rebuilding their blasted city. As a slow learner who too often sees certain slants of light poorly, I had no interest in ever returning to that charnel. Three years later, however, along with the nine hundred other Marines of the Fourth Marine Atomic Expeditionary Force, I crouched at the bottom of a five-foot-deep trench four thousand yards from Shot Hood. Shortly after witnessing the blast, we made a round trip back to Camp Mercury for a quick breakfast, thereby, we were told, allowing time for the irradiated residue of the mushroom and its stem to move off toward Utah. In mid-morning we marched in baking heat through bomb-triggered dust to within two hundred yards of ground zero. By the time we finished our maneuver we were covered with radioactive debris and looked forward to soap, showers, and clean clothes. As many of us would some day discover, our need was for something far more deeply cleansing than a shower.

Early in 1958 I left the Marines. Though still traumatized by what I had witnessed in the Nevada desert, I was fully engaged with the miracle of my son, born seven weeks before Shot Hood. Our leaders had ordered test participants never to discuss their experiences and, like most of my buddies, I tried to put Yucca Flat behind me. It was not to be. As a brand-new college student, I read *Hiroshima,* John Hersey's searing account of August 6, 1945, and its immediate aftermath. Because of Hersey's narrative skill, my own visit to the city, and my recent experience with the bomb, I dreamed and cried about that catastrophe. For months my nightmares wove together Yucca Flat and Hiroshima. At the same time, I was devastated to see so clearly how much I had missed in my 1954 journey and what a powerful opportunity my ignorance had caused me to squander. Though I didn't know how, and was confused about why, I sensed that someday, somehow, I would return to Hiroshima and the International Park for World Peace.

In early June 1981, accompanied by my partner Jane and sponsored by my friends at Japan's International Education System, I finally managed to return. I was immediately and powerfully struck by the changes that had occurred in the intervening twenty-seven years. By the time Jane and I left Hiroshima, I had come to grasp the Hibakusha's basic and, I believe, indisputable premise: Only through increased mutual understanding and acceptance can we hope to develop a deeper and more universal sense of brotherhood. And only through far greater brotherhood and international cooperation can the world hope to escape the ongoing horrors of modern warfare and threatened nuclear catastrophe.

Despite the obvious difficulties inherent in such a premise, the Peace Park is an inspired and inspiring reality. The seemingly miraculous ability of the Hibakusha to envision a collective future has allowed them to transcend individual despair. In 1981 their premise struck me as both true and unrealistic. Their vision is a thing of beauty. However, the idea that it was possible to recork the nuclear genie seemed little more than naïveté born of desperation. In some ways it still does.

Study, for example, the Doomsday Clock and the analysis behind it. Despite the end of the cold war, our world is becoming more dangerous, not less. On February 27, 2002, the editors of the *Bulletin of the Atomic Scientists* moved the big hand of the clock forward two minutes, setting it at seven minutes to midnight. This move toward nuclear midnight was the third since the end of the cold war in 1991. The editors' reasons for changing the time were that there has been insufficient progress toward nuclear disarmament; there is inadequate security for both nuclear weapons and fissionable materials; and the current administration prefers unilateral and preemptive actions, the pursuit of Star Wars, and the abandonment of the Antiballistic Missile Treaty. The editors are also concerned with increasing nuclear proliferation and the intensity of terrorism.[4]

Since that last resetting of the clock, the dangers have intensified, particularly in the Middle East, Asia, and even here at home, where the Bush administration is walking away from the Comprehensive Test Ban Treaty and preparing to resume nuclear testing at the Nevada Test Site.

The purposes of resumed testing include developing a "bunker-buster" atomic weapon that will penetrate deep, concrete-reinforced, enemy command centers, such as those manned not by terrorists but by seventy of our allies and trading partners around the planet; and developing small (under five-kiloton) atomic weapons for battlefield use. As it always has, the government maintains the often-disproved fiction that underground testing is completely safe and will pose no health risk for downwinders.[5]

Like the Hiroshima peace culture and all people everywhere who grasp the related issues of peace and justice, the atomic scientists know that "the growing inequality between rich and poor around the world...increases the potential for violence and war.... The success of the war on terrorism depends not only on disrupting and destroying terrorist organizations but also on eradicating the conditions that give rise to terror." The following statement, circulated by *Bulletin* sponsor John Polanyi and signed by 110 Nobel laureates, cuts to the core: "To survive in the world we have transformed, we must learn to think in a new way."[6]

"Life in the Dead Zone" is an eyewitness re-creation of the fear-induced tension and specific details experienced by this ex-Marine and his buddies at the Nevada Test Site between the seventeen-kiloton misfire of Shot Diablo on June 25, 1957, and the detonation of seventy-four-kiloton Shot Hood on July 5. The long narrative poem, "The Mourning Dove," focuses on the few minutes that immediately preceded and followed the shot and describes an incident mentioned in "Life in the Dead Zone."

"Collateral Damage" speaks briefly of the long-term damage experienced by atomic veterans, downwinders, test-site workers, and uranium miners. We were the expendable pawns of the cold war, those sacrificed in the name of national defense. This section also speaks of my own cancer and my attempts to turn an incurable and ultimately fatal disease to constructive use.

The second narrative poem, "The Survivor," was inspired by an encounter Jane and I had with one of the old women Hibakusha, a sweeper in the Peace Park. If "The Survivor" seems to reflect more despair than hope, it is because, despite all I had learned and felt, I took home with me from that 1981 journey a great deal of despair and very little hope.

In May 1993, increasingly aware that I had missed the essence of the Peace Park, I returned. Though still undiagnosed, I was already suffering from multiple myeloma, a once-rare but increasingly common form of ionizing radiation–induced bone–blood cancer. Though my 1993 journey began badly, I eventually found what I had earlier missed and sorely needed. The final narrative of this collection, "A Flight of Cranes," both integrates my previous three encounters with the bomb and distills the meaning of a return that came to be bathed in beauty.

In "A Flight of Cranes" I deal briefly with President Truman's decision to detonate Little Boy over Hiroshima and, three days later, to detonate Fat Man over Nagasaki. My concern here, however, is not so much with the events that led up to August 6 as with the question, "What now?" What, if anything, have we learned from Hiroshima and Nagasaki? And to what degree does that knowledge provide at least a modicum of hope for our future? Hiroshima's Peace Park speaks, mournfully but eloquently, to that subject. A more universal brotherhood rooted in peace and justice may yet prove to be illusory. Nevertheless, the vision and the hope do exist, centered in the new life and living practice that is the Hiroshima peace culture.

LEONARD BIRD
HIROSHIMA DAY, 2004

p a r t **o n e**

The national sacrifice

We either live together as brothers or we
are going to perish together as fools.
— MARTIN LUTHER KING JR.

The mourning dove

1.
Yucca Flat: 3:40 a.m., July 5, 1957:
Jury rigged along a desert trench
half a mile long, loudspeakers growl:
"Break ranks. Enter the trench."
And eight hundred pale Marines crawl
into trenches five feet deep, graves
for innocence, dug by machines
designed to claw sewer lines.
We stand within the trench, stand and shiver,
stand and wait. For the Word. For the dawn,
for seventy kilotons of fractured atoms.

❧ ❧ ❧

2.
4:00 a.m. Again the static-filled crackle
that rumbles like the gravelly voice of God:
"Gas masks in place. Breathe deep to check
the filter. Inspect the man behind."

4:30 a.m.: "Down on one knee. Pull your jacket
over your mask. Cover your face.
Bury your face in your crossed arms."
And wait. For the Word, for the dawn, for the Bomb.
Wait for the demented twist of that magic
gift Prometheus stole for man. Wait for man
to untwine the Alpha and Omega
to render his brilliant apocalypse.

4:39 a.m.: "One minute to detonation
and counting: 55... 54... 53..."
Four thousand yards from Ground Zero,
from that Faustian tower about to imitate
the sun, our brains constrict.
Our deepest fears condense to cold sweat.
"5... 4... 3... 2... 1..." A split second
that lasts a thousand years. And then
the white light, brighter than the desert sun,
burns through jackets pulled across taut faces,
burns through smoke-gray eyes of grotesque masks,
burns through pink tissue squinted shut, and burns
a nightmare image on the retina.

❊ ❊ ❊

3.
Again we wait. An eternity of silence
before the great KA-BOOM that rolls
across the buckling earth, a roll as slow

and deep as all the cannons of the world
massed for one last orgasm of war,
massed to celebrate the oft-prolonged
departure of a demented species.

We wait, cowering in that constricted pit
that borders hell. And then: An alien voice that jars
minds gone blank, the Titan voice growls,
"Stand up and face Ground Zero. Watch the fireball.
Watch the fireball. Watch the fireball..."
We stand, our eyes riveted
to the orange-black cloud. We stare,
green automatons wired to the ball of dust
that mushrooms toward the stratosphere.

Slowly, like a great bubble of muck,
the fireball swells and swells and swells,
rises, bloated, through the torn sky.
And then the winds begin, triggered
by the great cloud of bile that personifies
the eons of man's progress around the circle,
from cave to cave. Our mouths hang open.
Our eyes stare. Necks crane back until they
almost snap, as that earth-consuming mushroom
obscures the morning stars, blots out the sky,
then rains back upon the glowing earth
its man-concocted curse.

❧ ❧ ❧

4.

And once again, down the labyrinth of time,
that torn ghost still howls. And that speaker
still blares: "About face. Turn from the fireball.
Turn and leave the trench." That growl cracks
the stillness of hypnosis. The frozen line breaks.
Stunned Marines wriggle from the frothing trench.

I placed my hands upon the ledge and twisted
from the trench, just as the pale sun, not quite
obscured by a gray scrim of atomic dust,
rose above the far hills. But as my head
rose above the ledge, my outstretched hand grasped
a soft, spastic form. And as I touched, I saw
the bleeding dove, its feathers blasted by our
manmade sun. A torn mourning dove flopped,
twitched from spasm to spasm, its wings singed black.
I smelled the stink of charred flesh, a stench
as old as life, but rendered fresh by the wrath
of progress run amuck: Verdun, Warsaw,
Auschwitz, Hiroshima, Nagasaki,
and a hundred waiting towns whose tightly
woven strands of life our brilliant future
may too soon unwind.

❧ ❧ ❧

5.

That dove's melted eyes oozed gray pus.
And from a throat that had sung Man awake
since the dawn of time bubbled a faint
"squwik squwik squwik."
That mangled dove still smolders, radium
etched upon my soul. In my twisted dreams
that squeaking dove again becomes
the Holy Ghost, whose gray tears are shed
for man, for *homo ludens,* whose mad games
will someday self-destruct.

Life in the dead zone

June 25, 1957. Area 2b of the Nevada Test Site, seventy-five miles north of Las Vegas.

0405 hours: The twelve men of my squad talk quietly and stare down into the narrow, five-foot-deep trench that, we have repeatedly been told, will protect us from Shot Diablo, a seventeen-kiloton nuclear "device" perched atop an illuminated five-hundred-foot tower, thirty-five hundred yards to our north. I shake another cigarette from a pack of Camels and listen to the roar of our trucks as they shift into gear and speed south and away from the imminent blast.

Along with nine hundred other Marines, I have spent the past week wandering around this irradiated plain practicing war games, watching atomic-bomb training and propaganda films, and, in the searing heat, trying to stay awake through endless orientation lectures and pep talks. All the government cheerleading hasn't helped. Our bullshit detectors are too sensitized to deceit and hypocrisy.

0415 hours: From somewhere behind us a gravelly loud-speaker interrupts our reveries and quiet grousing: "Attention in the trenches! Attention in the trenches!"

I turn to the right and left, checking on my troops, two of whom are ignoring the command. "O'Donnell! Bronski! Can the bullshit and listen up."

"Yeah, Sarge. Sorry," Bronski mumbles.

"Enter the trench!" the loudspeaker commands in strong, staccato syllables. "Enter the trench! Enter the trench!" Quickly we hand our weapons to a buddy, place our palms on either side of the trench, lower ourselves into the dark earth, and reach up to grab our weapons. We stand four feet apart and look north into the darkness and the tall, illuminated tower that houses Shot Diablo.

0420 hours: "Ten minutes to detonation. Don your gas masks. Repeat: Don your gas masks."

"Here we go again," Bronski hisses. "I hate these fuckin' masks. Why do we have to put them on so soon?"

I start to say something, but Bronski is donning his mask even as he continues to grumble. We pull our tear-gas-stained, World War II masks from their sacks, remove our helmets, and adjust the clumsy and cracking rubber to our already sweating heads. Without being told, each man checks the straps and fit of the masked Marine to his right and left. I hear a mumbled, "Shit!" Two men over to my right, Corporal Washington is having trouble with O'Donnell's straps.

"What's the problem, Corporal?" I ask.

Washington holds the two straps that buckle the mask to a man's head. "Ain't no fuckin' buckle, Sarge."

"O'Donnell," I almost scream. O'Donnell is looking at his feet. His three-year hitch has been one disaster after another. "You shit for brains sorry ass excuse for a Marine. . . ." I stop myself. This is not the time or place for an ass reaming. "Tie the ends together, Washington. That should work. If not," I shrug, "the fallout is supposed to be harmless. Or so they say."

To my left, Corporal Begay lets loose with one of his cynical chuckles. "Yes, Bird. 'Or so they say.'"

0425 hours: "Five minutes to detonation. Assume the position. Repeat: Assume the position."

We've been through this drill a dozen times. But this one's for real. I turn on my flashlight and inspect the troops. No one has waited to be told twice. Within a minute each man is down on one knee, his jacket pulled over his head, his head buried in his crossed arms. "Be sure the trunk of your mask is free," I yell to my right and again to my left.

My mind turns to my seven-week-old son, and I wonder if I'll ever see him again. I'm hyperventilating and focus on slowing my breath. Gas masks require deep, even breathing.

My mind flashes back to July, three years earlier, and the train trip that Begay, Washington, and I took from Mishima to Hiroshima. Until coming to Nevada I've thought little about that journey, which I resented taking and had blocked from my mind as soon as it was over. I remember the children squatting listlessly in front of their four-foot-tall hovels, watching silently as the three of us strode by. One of the little girls had a baby strapped to her back, where I now see my son's smiling face. I shake my head to end the memory and curse the sweat building inside my gas mask.

0429 hours: "One minute to detonation," the loudspeaker blares. "Hold your positions!" I fall to one knee, pull my jacket up over my head, bury my face in my crossed arms, and wait for the loud click that signals detonation.

"Five... four... three... two... one..."

I hold my breath, waiting for the click and what will follow. But there is no click.

Time halts. For an endless minute I hear little but my own rapid and shallow breathing. I try to take deeper breaths but can't. When I hear cries and curses, I pull my mask away and, keeping my head well below the top of the trench, scream, "Hold your positions! Hold your positions!"

I can smell the fear. The loudspeaker is silent. I open my eyes and shine my light up and down the trench. Though everyone is still bent over and holding position, bodies are shifting uneasily.

"What's wrong, Sarge?" someone mumbles through the heavy cotton of his jacket.

"How the hell should I know? Hold the position!" I pull my jacket back over my face and bend over as my own terror knots my stomach.

0433 hours: "Misfire! Misfire!" the voice behind the loudspeaker screams. "Keep calm in the trenches and stay down. Misfire! Repeat: Misfire!" The fear behind the voice sends a charge of adrenaline along the trench. Somewhere to my left someone sobs and someone else curses: "Your bawling ain't helping one goddamn bit, jerk off."

"Give him a pacifier," Orsky says.

I hear a couple of nervous laughs just as the loudspeaker again clicks on and a different voice speaks, this one slow and calm, resonant with reassurance. "We have experienced a misfire. There is no apparent danger. You may move around in the trench. The smoking lamp is lighted. But be sure to keep your heads well below the parapet."

Almost as one, we rip off helmets and sweat-filled masks and lean back to inhale huge gulps of desert air.

"Hey, Bird. Can I bum a smoke?"

I nod at Begay, the brightest man in the outfit but still only a corporal after almost five years in the Corps. Begay is a "lifer," totally alienated from his Navajo family and any thought of ever again returning to civilian life. We light our smokes and try to relax, despite the presence of a misfired atomic bomb sitting on a tower less than two miles away.

"What do you think went wrong?" I ask.

"I don't know. Maybe an electrical failure that broke the signal so it never reached the bomb," Begay shrugs. "Maybe the bomb's a dud."

"It's not a bomb, Begay. It's a 'device.'"

"If that seventeen-kiloton hummer had gone off, you'd have thought 'device.'" Begay looks at me like I'm an idiot. I've seen the look before, had to face it for days after he, Washington, and I returned from Hiroshima three years earlier.

To Begay's disgust I had griped to our tent mates that there was nothing there to see, just a bunch of ruins and homeless people and a new park with small trees and a few monuments—a long train ride for nothing, nothing but a wasted weekend and a good head of confusion and depression.

Washington plops down next to us, leans his head back, and gazes at the fading morning stars. "What do you all think? Will we get to go home now?"

I shake my head. "Who knows?"

"No way," Begay says. "The brass brought us out here to be guinea pigs for one of their big bombs. As soon as they figure out what happened with Diablo, we'll be right back in these trenches. Different day but same time, same stations, same Diablo."

"Man, I do hope you are wrong," Washington almost whispers. "I don't want to do this again."

❧ ❧ ❧

Yucca Flat, Area 9a of the Nevada Test Site. Independence Day, 1957, shortly after noon.

Our mile-long convoy of Marine-green trucks cuts across the heart of a heat- and bomb-blasted desert. The speeding trucks huddle together like an infantry patrol succumbing to its most dangerous instinct. Through the heat waves we see chains of low mountains to the east and west. I stare at the black road and at the gray shadows cast by the nuclear light of some previous blast. Though the sun is directly overhead, the sharp negative shadows of the passing utility poles slice across the highway at a thirty-degree angle.

"Remember those shadows in Hiroshima?" I ask, pointing at the asphalt.

"Yeah, Sarge," Washington mutters. "That guy against the wall?"

I nod. "The bomb that shadowed this road was a lot smaller than what we're now scheduled to see."

"Yes, 'see,'" Begay says quietly. "See, hear, breathe, taste, touch. This thing could kill us."

"No shit, Dick Tracy," Washington mumbles. That ends the discussion. Except for Orsky at the head of the bench, who talks to himself, and Mendoza's lisping Hail Marys, there is only the hum of the tires on the baking-hot black highway.

Begay is wrong about us hanging around for Diablo. Would that he had been right. As frightening as Diablo is scheduled to be, Shot Hood looks to be far worse. And Hood is where we're headed. Rumor has it that Hood is a monster bomb, a thermonuclear bomb, which means an H-bomb.

I think back to our artillery base on the treeless north flank of Mt. Fuji and to the weekend that Begay dragged us off to Hiroshima. On the way from the train station to the new International Peace Park, we passed a chilling landmark. Etched on a dark granite wall was the negative shadow of a man at the instant of his atomic disintegration. The shadow seemed to be seated, its head bowed as if in prayer.

"We're leaving the asphalt," someone yells. I stand and turn to the front of the truck. The leading vehicle veers northeast along a two-rut dirt road that cuts across an upward-sloping plain. The yucca are thicker here, or at least once were.

Much of the land and its scant vegetation have been badly charred by previous blasts.

The convoy crosses a spine of low hills and heads for ground zero, where we come to a halt at the base of a five-hundred-foot tower. Thick cables stretch straight up from its top for more than a thousand feet and anchor a large silver balloon. Though awed by the sheer height of the contraption, we gaze out into the desert. A thousand yards beyond ground zero is spread an assemblage of surplus military equipment— tanks, trucks, howitzers, even a cherry-picker crane, the kind of equipment we know, love, and curse.

Jamison, the top sergeant, leaps from his jeep and yells, "This is it, men. Hit the deck and fall in. Move it!" Within two minutes the battalion of uneasy Marines has formed an open horseshoe and stands at ease facing the black tower.

"So this is Yucca Flat," Begay whispers.

"Yeah," I reply with unconscious reverence. "And that there balloon is Shot Hood."

"Do tell," Washington mimics, his gaze climbing the tower and the tethered balloon.

From the end of the convoy, a second jeep weaves its way forward and brakes to a halt next to Jamison's. An overweight Army colonel carrying a megaphone, and a goggle-eyed civilian sporting a safari jacket climb from the jeep and saunter up to Jamison, who salutes sharply, turns to us, and barks, "Listen up!"

The colonel steps forward and clears his throat. "Good afternoon, Marines. My name is Colonel Saxon. I am a nuclear-warfare specialist attached to Camp Mercury. My civilian colleague here is Dr. Phillips, a radiation specialist. You volunteers are here to help simulate the nuclear battle-field."

"What's the man talking about?" Washington mumbles. "We was volunteered."

"Yes," Begay agrees. "Volunteered. Guinea pigs one and all. Nothing but expendable props."

The colonel rambles on, "Because the godless Communists now have the bomb, we must assume the worst and test our own weapons in battlefield simulations. That means with live troops present. For Shot Hood, Operation Plumbbob, you Marines are the live troops." He turns to the civilian. "Dr. Phillips?"

Phillips takes a step forward and clears his throat. "At 0440 hours tomorrow morning, we will detonate a seventy-four-kiloton nuclear device. This device is roughly six times the size of the one we detonated above Hiroshima. The two-stage blast will destroy much if not most of the surplus equipment you see spread out beyond the tower. It will also create considerable amounts of contaminated dust. The dust poses no immediate danger. In any case, you will be wearing gas masks." The physicist stops and looks at the colonel, who motions him to continue, but Phillips merely shakes his head, as if disclaiming both knowledge and responsibility.

The colonel shrugs and continues, "This will be your dry run. Since you were in trenches last week for the Diablo misfire, and since you've all seen films of Hiroshima and Nagasaki, you are all wondering about your safety. Right?" Up and down the line, young Marines greet his question with a low, confused rumble of awe and fear tinged with anger.

"At ease, Marines!" Jamison barks.

Colonel Saxon saunters along the line, confident of our total attention. "Stand assured! You will be at no risk." The physicist stares at the ground and shuffles his feet. "None whatsoever," the colonel repeats. "*If* you follow our every instruction." That reassurance triggers another low rumble from the troops.

"Uh oh!" Begay whispers. "You know what 'none whatsoever' means."

"Yeah. Bend over, grab your ankles, and wait for the shaft," I answer.

"The junkyard out there stretches six thousand yards from ground zero," the colonel continues. "In addition to testing the effects on troops in close proximity to a nuclear detonation, we want to study the effects of blast and heat. Hence the junk. You will learn more soon."

"Yeah! I bet," Washington snickers.

After a few hundred more words of government wisdom and reassurance, the colonel heads back to his jeep, the physicist following like a tethered hound. Jamison orders us into skirmish lines and moves us north into the junkyard, where we pass and casually inspect surplus equipment awaiting nuclear demolition.

Four thousand yards out from ground zero we stop at a series of long trenches, twins to those we crouched in for

Diablo, two feet wide and five feet deep, as if the brass are running parallel sewer lines across the Nevada desert.

"This is it?" someone yells. "Jesus Christ Almighty!"

"Yeah, right," I mumble. I don't know what we expected—maybe a deeper trench, maybe a sandbag parapet, certainly something more protective than a pit like the one we hid in for what was to have been a far smaller bomb. Only four thousand yards away, we can actually see the contraption that might waste us.

From invisible hiding places on the far side of a low hill, loudspeakers blare, "*Enter the trench!*" Four gravelly staccato beats and then a long, humming pause: "*Enter the trench! Enter the trench!*" Amid some grumbled anger and obscene wit, we climb into the pit and wait an interminable half hour for the next order.

When the record finally stops, the colonel's proud tones resonate through the loudspeakers. "Early tomorrow you will enter these trenches, don gas masks, and prepare for the blast. You will probably hear the click that detonates the device. Even with your eyes closed and covered by your gas mask and field jacket, you will experience a blinding flash of light followed by a second even more intense light that will continue for some time. Shortly after, an enormous explosion will roll over your trench. For the few short seconds of silence before the racket of the implosion rolls back, you could find yourself in a vacuum. Shortly after the implosion, you will stand up and face ground zero. You will observe the effects of the fireball and its subsequent mushroom. Approximately two hours later, you will mount an assault on ground zero, where you will participate in an exercise designed to study the aftereffects of a nuclear detonation. At no time will you be in significant danger. We will now practice. Don your masks!"

Late that evening, back in our squad tents, we lie on our canvas cots, smoking and rehashing both the practice run and the films we'd seen about Hiroshima and Nagasaki. The thermometer in the tent reads 98 degrees Fahrenheit, but it feels hotter. Except for Begay, Washington, and me, everyone in the tent is quiet, trying to ward off heat and fear through sleep or a fast read. O'Donnell and Bardin have pillows over their heads, as if trying to block out our conversation.

Washington strikes a match for his fourth cigarette in an hour, pauses, shakes his head, and says, "What I just can't understand, man, is how come they're looking for the blast to burn mannequins in a machine-gun nest at six thousand yards out, but say they ain't no harm going to come to us at four thousand yards."

"We'll be at the bottom of a trench," I say. "The dummies won't."

"Think about it, Bird," Begay says. He's lying on his back. Every thirty seconds, like a slow-beat metronome, his arm rises, bends, and places his smoke in his mouth. He takes a deep drag, lets the arm fall back to his side, exhales slowly, and says, "The brass rates Diablo at seventeen kilotons, and Hood at seventy-four kilotons. Hood is roughly 450 percent larger than Diablo. And they're going to put us four thousand yards from the blast, rather than thirty-five hundred. Do the math."

"So what's the point?"

"The point is, the brass get a far bigger bang for their war games, and we get a chintzy 14 percent increase in 'protection.' The point is, in Hiroshima 12.5-kiloton Little Boy destroyed damn near everything within a radius of two kilometers. What will Hood do?"

"Yeah, well," I respond lamely. "Tomorrow we'll do what we're told, just as we always have, whether the brass knows what it's doing or not. Let's talk about something else."

"Think about it, Bird. Washington has a point."

"Yeah, and I have another point, Sarge," Washington says, lighting a fresh cigarette with the one he's just finishing. "What about the fallout? What did that science dude mean when he say, 'no immediate harm'?"

"Just what he said," I respond, though struck by Washington's focus on the implications of "immediate."

"We know a lot more about fallout than that scientist was willing to talk about." Begay cocks his head and gives me another one of his "Bird, you are an idiot" looks. "You never did read that book I gave you, did you?"

Though I know what he means, I say, "What book?"

"*Hiroshima*. John Hersey's book." Begay gives me another look and launches into a rehash of our visit to Hiroshima and all that we saw and learned there. The last thing I want right now is more morbid monologues. I pull myself from my cot and wander out into the night. "By the way, Bird," Begay chuckles as I exit the tent, "Happy Independence Day."

I walk through the long lines of canvas squad tents out toward the camp perimeter, stop in the middle of a thin yucca patch, and look around. To the south a soft glow rises from the lights of Las Vegas, some seventy miles distant. I lift my head, turn a slow 360, and stare into a clean sky. Venus has long since sunk in the West; within a few hours it will rise in the East to announce our nuclear D Day. I turn and face north, toward the tower. Almost directly overhead, the long arc of the Milky Way trails a cape of crystal dust. I follow the lines of the Dipper to Polaris, which hangs over Utah like an announcement.

I am a twenty-one-year-old sergeant in the U.S. Marine Corps, seven months from discharge and anxious to be gone from the Corps. I am also the father of a brand-new son and have never felt so proud—or so vulnerable. Despite the lingering heat, I'm shivering. I hear a rustling sound and freeze. A jackrabbit dashes from beneath a mesquite bush and speeds across the open desert to a Joshua tree. A whistling nighthawk dives almost to the top of the tall cactus before veering away. My stomach seizes and I fall to my knees and vomit next to a small red patch of Indian paintbrush. I hang my head between my arms and spit and retch until my stomach feels like it's clawing up through my throat. Finally, turning weakly away from the sour stench, I try to slow my shallow breathing and take deep breaths. In deep. Out slow. In deep.

For the first time since giving thanks for the birth of my son, I try to pray, but fail to carve my dread into words. After mumbling "Please, God, please, God, please, God" ceaselessly for a long time, I sit back and stare again at the great sweep of the Milky Way. I mutter fragments of the Lord's Prayer, a few Hail Marys I learned from a Catholic girlfriend, and a lot more "Please, Gods." After a dozen more deep breaths, I rise to my feet and wander back to the squad tent.

✧ ✧ ✧

Yucca Flat, July 5, 0400 hours.

We drop into our narrow trench shortly after 0300 hours. A long half-dozen cigarettes later, the loudspeakers begin their intrusive dirge: "Don your gas masks; check your straps. Check your buddy's straps. Fall to one knee. Cover your eyes. Pull your field jacket over your head and over your face. Cross your arms on your knee. Bury your face in your crossed arms." After a few minutes, the record starts over. Again and again we don our masks and move nervously through the drill.

At 0415 the record stops and a real voice blares, "At ease in the trenches, Marines. Twenty-five minutes until detonation. The smoking lamp is lighted." For the next quarter hour we try to relax. Some of the troops squat in the bottom of the trench, masking fear with the grossest jokes they know. Some pray openly while others stare at their feet and mumble. Most of us remain standing to smoke one last cigarette after another and peer toward the silver light of the illuminated balloon four thousand yards away in the predawn darkness.

A new voice blares from the loudspeakers. "Attention in the trenches! The time is 0430 hours. Ten minutes until zero hour. The smoking lamp is out." The voice is deeper, stern, each staccato clause gravelly with command. We take last deep drags from our smokes and lower our voices, as if even our whispers might trigger the monster prematurely.

"Jesus Christ!" Two men to my right, Washington's rich voice sounds more like a prayer than a curse. Ten minutes! I think. The trench closes in and my mind shuts down. I concentrate on deep breathing and start counting. Just past two hundred, I feel a great need to relieve my bladder. Like several others up and down the trench, I unbutton my fatigues, lean against the wall, and piss into the compacted sand.

"Stand by! The time is 0335 hours. Five minutes to detonation." The voice sounds proud, as if it is the creator of all that is about to engulf us. "The clock is running. Stand by!"

Stand by! As if we are about to climb from our trenches and flee, though I know in my every cell—and will always know—that fleeing is precisely what we should do. Instead, like soft-eyed beagles under the surgeon's knife at Animal Testing, Inc., we wait, numb and impotent.

"Four minutes to zero hour. Don your gas masks. This is not a drill. Repeat! This is not a drill. Don your masks. Check your straps. Check your buddy. Check your filter. Repeat! Don your gas masks. Check...!" I shiver. Men wearing gas masks sound like last-gasp asthmatics.

"Three minutes until detonation. Check your straps. Check your buddy. Check your filter. Fall to one knee. Assume the position. Stand by."

Inhale. Exhale. *Huuuuugh. Whooooosssshh. Huuuuugh. Whooooosssshh.* Our forced breaths rise through gasping lungs and open, wet mouths like echoes in a skintight sound chamber. *Huuuugh. Whooosssh.* I turn my head to the right and left and peer through the smoke-gray lenses. Each of the twelve men in my squad is already in the position. Like one-kneed fetuses, they have wrapped themselves in their field jackets and buried their heads in their arms. I reach my hands back and pull my jacket up over my head and masked face, fall to one knee, rest my chin on my crossed arms, and suck raspy breath through the carbon filter. And wait.

"Two minutes until zero hour. Two minutes! Assume the final position. Cover your faces. Block out all light. Cross your arms on your knee. Bury your covered face in your crossed arms. Repeat! Block out all light!"

I check and recheck for light but make sure the trunk of my mask hangs free. Despite the predawn chill, I am already sweating.

"One minute to detonation. Fifty-five, fifty-four, fifty-three."

The mask smells like old inner tubes tainted with tear gas. My breaths rise and fall like boomers crashing on the cliffs of some nightmare sea. I am alone, adrift in total darkness, like a vibrating particle awaiting the Big Bang. *Huuuuggh. Whhooooosssh.*

"Twenty-six, twenty-five, twenty-four."

Four thousand yards from ground zero, from that Faustian tower about to imitate the sun, our brains condense to cold sweat.

"Five, four, three, two, one..."

From the direction of the tower I hear a sharp click. Night

disappears. A white sun burns through crossed arms, cotton jackets, rubber masks, and tightly closed eyes. Then the light seems to intensify before slowly fading to lighter shades of green and yellow.

Again we wait, our shoulders braced against the sides of the trench. After a silent second that stretches past eternity, the blast crashes by, two feet above our bowed heads. The vacuum behind the explosion tries to suck us from the trench. Up and down the line, walls collapse. In that short space before the great roar of imploded matter, desperate shouts echo along the line. And then the second blast, the most thunderous *KKKKKK-rrakkKK* of imploding matter that America has ever felt, rolls back over our bowed heads.

To my right the collapsing trench muffles screams of fright and calmer cries for help. I pull my jacket back, open my eyes, and peer at a wall of swirling dust where Begay should be. Keeping low, I take two cautious steps and trip over his bent back. Begay is on his knees, digging at a steep slope of collapsed sand that has knocked Washington to the ground. Washington's yells seep through the sand. I try to help, but the trench is too narrow. "Use your helmet!" I yell. Begay rips off his helmet and bales furiously. One of Washington's arms flails above the sand like the desperate wave of a man going down for the third time. I lean over Begay's back, grab the waving arm, and pull, leaning back with all my strength. Slowly, Washington's covered head emerges from the sand. Begay grabs his shoulder and we pull him back to a kneeling position. Begay pushes Washington's jacket back from his head and yells, "Breathe! You're clear! Breathe!" Washington's chest heaves. Through the dusty, gray lenses his brown eyes are round with panic. "Breathe! Breathe!"

Washington rips off his mask, takes three great gasps and, seeing the beige air we are breathing, crams his mask back against his face. "Okay," he finally squeaks. "I'm okay."

The dirt storm engulfs us. I turn to my right and left and yell at the top of my lungs, Third Squad! Sound off!" A minute later, satisfied that my Marines are okay, I succumb to my fear. Every muscle in my body as stiff as dried bones, I wrap my arms around my legs and cower in the bottom of the trench, tighten my butt, and somehow will my bowels not to move.

"Attention in the trenches!" The titanic voice blasts through our heads. "Stand up and face ground zero! Watch the fireball! Stand up and face ground zero! Watch the fireball!"

I hold my fetal position for a few more seconds, then place my open palms against the cool sand wall and push myself to my feet. In the faint dawn an orange-black tornado howls. Our mouths hang open. Like green automatons wired to ground zero, we stare at the rising ball of red and orange and yellow atomic matter, already ten thousand feet above the desert floor. Twenty thousand feet. Our mesmerized faces tilt back as the great cloud of nuclear bile becomes our umbrella. For fifteen speechless minutes we watch the fireball rise through the torn sky like a great bubble of enflamed muck. Beyond forty thousand feet the mushroom blots out the morning stars and rains down veils of poison ash.

"Attention in the trenches!" The amplified growl cracks the stillness of mass hypnosis. I put my hands over my ears and shut my eyes. "Attention! Leave the trenches and fall into formation. Prepare to move out. Repeat. Leave the trenches!"

Gas masks still in place and taking shallow, frightened breaths, the battalion wriggles from the trenches just as the pale sun, not quite obscured by a gray scrim of atomic dust, rises above a low line of barely visible hills.

As my head rises above the trench, my groping hand touches a bleeding mourning dove, its feathers blasted by the heat. "LOOOOKKK!" I scream. "Goddamn!" Within seconds a score of us stand in a semicircle and stare at our feet, where the torn dove flops and twitches. We smell the stink of charred flesh. Melted eyes ooze gray pus, and from the throat of this scorched, twitching dove bubbles nothing but a faint "sqwick sqwick sqwick."

Two hours later, after a round trip to Camp Mercury and a quick breakfast that many of us couldn't touch, and already sweating in the July heat, we ride numbly back toward ground zero. When the leading jeep breasts the low ridge of the hogback, the driver slows to stare. The driver and the colonel don their gas masks. No one in the following convoy waits to be told. We hurriedly cram our faces into our gray rubber masks and stare into the poison web of man's latest Armageddon.

Though we are still several miles from the hypocenter of the blast, all we see before us is desolation. Many of the

Joshua trees and yucca still burn. Most have been blown over by the nuclear wind. All across the plain, columns of black smoke spiral toward the murky sky. We pass scores of dead and dying birds and rabbits and even two coyotes. We gawk at a few rabbits, obviously blind, running in straight lines until they carom off rocks or smoking stumps. Within three miles of ground zero all signs of life, or even recognizable death, have disappeared. At ground zero and for at least half a mile in any direction, nothing exists but a concave disk of blowing dirt.

From the head of the convoy the word passes back to dismount. We form open skirmish lines and stare beyond the ruined military equipment toward the not-so-distant trenches where we had huddled a few short hours before.

"All right, Marines!" Jamison yells. "We're going to take a little stroll through the junkyard to survey the damage. Keep your eyes open. As hot as it already is, you may not be able to wear your masks very long, but do your damnedest! Move out!" Jamison brushes the accumulating dust from his fatigues and leads us north toward a Sherman tank a few hundred yards away.

After a few yards, "Hope we're not... any of this shit," Washington yells, his words muffled by his mask.

"What?" I yell back. "What's wrong?"

Behind the gray lenses, Washington's brown eyes gleam with fright. "Hope we don't breathe any of this dust," he says slowly, distinctly.

Though I breathe deeply and taste nothing but the stale trace of tear gas, Washington's fear burns, as if he has jabbed me with a cattle prod. "That's what we have masks for," I reply, shaking my head and moving forward.

Within minutes, however, the lenses of my mask are so covered with sweat and fog that I can't see. Already breath comes hard. Halfway to the Sherman tank I have to stop and lift my mask to gulp air. Many of the troops have already removed their gas masks. Shortly I have to stop again, aware that, wearing the mask, I cannot both breathe and move forward.

Though my eyes are shut, I hear Begay laugh. "Take it off, Bird. You think these puny masks are gonna stop those radioactive zits?"

"Yeah. Well. That's what the brass says," I mutter.

Washington shakes his head in disbelief. "Begay says it's gonna take a few years to know, and Begay studied physics in college."

I look across at Begay, who shrugs, "Time will tell."

The blast has slung the tank a good hundred yards and slammed it back to earth, where it lies on its side, half buried in the swirling sand. Fifty yards beyond, a broken tank tread curls around a rock like a huge snake. Even Jamison and the officers seem dumbstruck. When they decide to move us along, Jamison just shakes his head and strides silently north.

Spread over an area the size of a football field lie the torn, sandblasted pieces of a large truck. A few hundred yards beyond the truck, maybe two thousand yards from ground zero, a cherry-picker crane still rests on its collapsed cab, but its long, erect neck and defiant beak have collapsed. Rather than two straight lines of latticed steel joined like the legs of a compass, the blasted neck and beak have collapsed into two twisted curves. The arm, maybe twenty feet long, has wrapped itself around the cab; the shorter beak, half melted, droops to the ground like a strand of overcooked spaghetti.

Roughly three thousand yards out from the hypocenter, bundles of charred flora become recognizable, and we again run into the charred remnants of birds, rabbits, and rodents.

Four thousand yards out, we leap across our trenches and keep heading south. We encounter our most numbing sight six thousand yards from ground zero. Mannequins dressed in Marine-green fatigues and camouflaged helmets appear to stare out from behind the sandbagged parapet of a long, shallow trench. The dummies crouch behind machine guns, as if ordered to be the last defense against the blast. The dummies' collars and cuffs are charred and their plastic faces contorted beyond recognition by seventy-four kilotons of nuclear heat.

"That's us," Washington whispers. "Six thousand yards out and still barbecued."

Half an hour later we march over a low hill and see our waiting trucks parked in neat formation a hundred yards from a lone Quonset hut. We line up in open-platoon formation, two steps between ranks and two steps apart. The loudspeaker atop the Quonset clicks on, and the voice that had an eternity earlier ordered us through the Big Blast again speaks: "All right, Marines. Dust yourselves off. Thoroughly. Repeat. Thoroughly!"

As soon as the speaker clicks back off, Jamison yells, "Get those damn masks back on before you dust off!" an order everybody rushes to obey. We put our masks back on and brush each other vigorously. When Jamison removes his mask, we do the same. Almost in unison, we rip off our masks and take long, deep breaths of polluted air. The sage and rabbit brush smell far better than I remembered.

"At ease," the loudspeakers growl. "The smoking lamp is lighted." Everyone who smokes and a few who don't immediately light up and wait for what is yet to come.

Ten minutes later a platoon of Army corporals carrying long-handled Geiger counters, and a second platoon of privates wielding house brooms appear from behind the Quonset and head our way. Every Marine's head cranes to the right, mesmerized by the approaching Geiger counters. I can hear one coming even before it gets to Begay, two men and twelve feet to my right. "*Kleeq-kleeq-kleeq-kleeq-kleeq.*" I shiver. "What the fuck are we supposed to do if we're too hot?" I ask the Army corporal as he approaches Washington.

The corporal turns to me and spits a wad of tobacco juice. "Take a shower and get some new duds, sucker." Holding the flat plate of the counter a foot from Washington's body, he starts at his feet and moves slowly up his body to his head and back down to his feet, where the counter clicks wildly.

"Sweeper!" the corporal yells, then steps back. A private takes a straw house broom to Washington, who turns his head and protects his face with his arms. When the dust dissipates, the corporal steps back in and goes over Washington again. The counter seems about half a decibel quieter. The corporal nods and moves on to me.

The counter changes from a whine to a scream, first at my feet and lower legs, then again as it passes my groin. *"KLEEQ-KLEEQ-KLEEQ-kleeq-kleeq-kleeq-kleeq-KLEEQ-KLEEQ-KLEEQ."* The pattern repeats on the way back down.

"Sweeper!" the corporal yells. I close my eyes, cover my face, and wait while the rough straw brushes my body. The Geiger counter screams. "Again!" the corporal orders. I recover my face and hyperventilate. Again the counter screams.

"All right, buddy. Open your eyes," the corporal says. "Shower time. Report to the east end of the Quonset. Sorry." And then he moves on to the next man. Stunned, I move out of formation and head for the Quonset, where I squeeze into a room full of quiet, frightened Marines, strip away my contaminated fatigues and wait, naked and shivering. As soon as there is space I step into the shower and scrub every inch of skin and scalp, soaping and scrubbing until my skin glows pink.

Once showered and dressed in new fatigues, I step out into the midday sun and fall into formation between Washington and Begay. While waiting for the last few stragglers to emerge from the showers, we stand quietly and stare out beyond ground zero toward Utah. On the far horizon heat waves shimmer above a thin mirage of blue.

Collateral Damage

When caught up in the angst of significant events, we tend to remember where we were and why. During the largest atmospheric blast ever to be unleashed over this continent, I crouched in a trench four thousand yards from ground zero. In the last agonizing hours of the Cuban Missile Crisis, I was part of a large group clustered around a radio in the University of Utah union. I learned of John F. Kennedy's assassination while skiing at Alta, and watched the fall of the Berlin Wall on CNN. I heard of the coup that toppled Gorbachev while fishing with my son, David, in the San Juan Mountains of southern Colorado. September 11 hit the first morning my wife Jane and I spent in our new home. And when America invaded Iraq and initiated "Shock and Awe," I was recovering from a bone-marrow transplant.

We tend to limit our sense of catastrophe to visibly dramatic events, such as the cataclysms of nature and the horrors of war and genocide. To such events we often react with compassion and charity. We seem, unfortunately, far less able to deal with events that lie beyond or seem to contradict the clamoring demands of our short-term interests and fascinations. We tend to ignore, sublimate, or deny slower-acting, less visible, and more abstract threats to our survival. Global warming is one example. Ionizing radiation is another.

The effects of nuclear and thermonuclear blast and fire on people and property are immediate and stunningly dramatic. Ionizing radiation and fallout, however, are invisible, slow to act, and difficult to evaluate, but ultimately destructive of human and animal life. Although we are only beginning to understand the poisons of ionizing radioactivity, all that we do know is bad. There is *no* safe level of radiation.[7] It accumulates in our blood and bones. The danger lies hidden, the antithesis of all that is dramatic and attention-riveting. For those invested in continued atomic-weapons development, the effects are also easy to deny.

❧ ❧ ❧

Many Americans still don't understand. The so-called National Sacrifice Area was ostensibly limited to the underpopulated ranching and farming communities of southern Utah, eastern Nevada, and the Arizona strip. The hard truth speaks otherwise. The area of contamination extends far beyond the American Southwest. Nor are the sacrifices limited to Navajo uranium miners, enlisted guinea pigs, and Mormon sheepherders. We are *all* downwinders. We now know that radiation poison traveled on the prevailing winds and at different altitudes. Sometimes the mushroom went one way and the stem another, as in the map of my exercise, Shot Hood.[8]

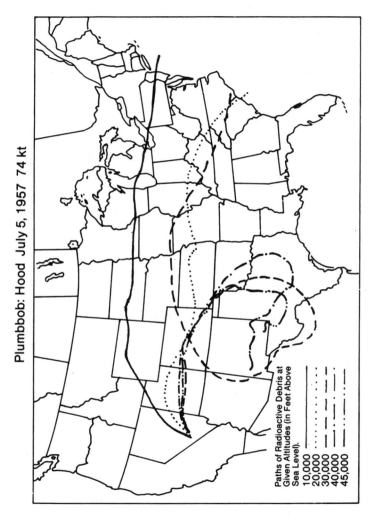

Plumbbob: Hood July 5, 1957 74 kt

Paths of Radioactive Debris at Given Altitudes (in Feet Above Sea Level).

10,000
20,000
30,000
40,000
45,000

FIGURE 1. Plumbbob: Shot Hood, July 5, 1957, 74 kt. From Richard L. Miller, *Under the Cloud: The Decades of Nuclear Testing*, 462. Reprinted by permission.

For twelve years the clouds of contaminated particles crossed the country, usually but not always on the prevailing westerly winds. In addition to poisoning the upper Southwest, the resulting fallout created "hot spots" from Salt Lake City to Grand Junction, Colorado, to Dallas, Texas, to Albany, New York—affecting scores of innocent communities in between. As an example, Albany, New York, ranked third in deposits of iodine-131 during the period of atmospheric testing.[9]

Far less notorious, but nevertheless lethal, underground detonations continued. Between 1962 and 1992 there were 804 such detonations. Fifty-four percent of these presumably safe experiments leaked, some seriously.[10] As deadly as the atmospheric tests were, venting underground detonations spewed even more poisoned particulates into the atmosphere than did the aboveground tests. Basically, underground and at-ground detonations suck up more particulate matter and hence have more debris to deposit. For example, while Shot Sedan was detonated 535 feet beneath the surface and Shot Banebury 900 feet underground, both leaked massive amounts of radiation into the atmosphere.[11]

For twenty-five years after the cessation of atmospheric testing, the government and its in-house scientists denied that fallout presented any danger to human beings—this despite what we had learned about cancer rates among the Hibakusha, the atomic-bomb survivors of Hiroshima and Nagasaki. Finally, in response to various class-action lawsuits from the National Association of Atomic Veterans, other veterans' groups, and civilian downwinders, in 1983 the government admitted a number of cancers to be related to ionizing radiation. In subsequent years and as the result of continued lawsuits and negative publicity for the government, a few other cancers have been added.[12] In 1990 Congress passed, and President George H. W. Bush signed, the Radiation Exposure Compensation Act (RECA), which provided financial compensation to sufferers of the eighteen "allowed" cancers. Continued lawsuits and the attendant publicity forced the opening of hitherto-classified documents, documents that demonstrated the self-aggrandizing perfidy of the Atomic Energy Commission and its successor, the Department of Energy.[13]

By 1990 many of the potential beneficiaries of the RECA were dead, some long dead. Moreover, the RECA presumed that the nuclear poisons had somehow miraculously stopped when they reached southern Utah, eastern Nevada, and a thin strip of northern Arizona. If you were one of that scant population during the appropriate dates and were being eaten by one of the cancers specified, the RECA would bestow upon you or your survivor the munificent sum of $50,000 for pain, suffering, and loss.[14] Even for those survivors, the paperwork can be daunting. As for those of us who live outside the contaminated area? The prevailing winds are southwesterly. Most of western and large parts of eastern America have been long contaminated. Richard L. Miller's map illustrates this pointedly.[15] Again, we are all downwinders.

Among the RECA eligibles are about 230,000 armed forces personnel. By the time the RECA became relevant, however, more than twenty thousand of these atomic veterans,

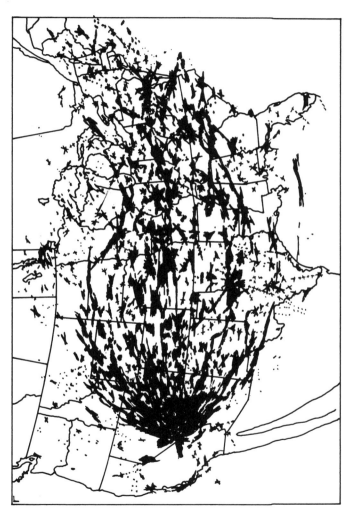

FIGURE 2. Areas of the Continental United States Crossed by More Than One Nuclear Cloud from Aboveground Detonations. From Richard L. Miller, *Under the Cloud: The Decades of Nuclear Testing*, 444. Reprinted by permission.

who were less than fifty years old, had died. And like the initial survivors of Hiroshima and Nagasaki, test survivors continue to experience abnormally high incidences of diseases related to radiation poisoning, particularly from the effects of cesium-137, plutonium, strontium-80, strontium-90, and iodine-131.[16] For example, the veterans of Operation Plumbbob suffer from sterility and various blood and bone cancers such as leukemia and multiple myeloma at four times the expected rate for men of their generation, and from polycythemia vera—a rare, premalignant disease of the bone marrow— at more than one hundred times the expected rate.[17]

My cancer is multiple myeloma, a once rare but increasingly common form of bone–blood cancer related to plutonium, strontium-90, and cesium-137, all of which attack bone. During the first tracking of downwinders (1958-66), the rate of new multiple myeloma diagnoses was 1.6 times the expected average. By the second tracking period (1972-80), the rate of new myeloma cases had increased to 3.5 times the expected average.[18]

Multiple myeloma is an exceedingly slow-onset cancer. Had there been a later tracking period, the ratio would have been even higher. Significant pockets of multiple myeloma did not show up in Hiroshima and Nagasaki until the early 1980s, almost forty years after Little Boy and Fat Man.[19]

Starting with a broken chromosome or two as the result of some form of environmental contamination, particularly ionizing radiation, multiple myeloma can hide in the bone marrow and multiply slowly for decades before manifesting

	1957–66	1972–80
Leukemia	5.3[††]	3.5
Lymphoma	—	1.9
Thyroid cancer	4.3	8.2
Breast cancer	—	1.9
Colon cancer	—	1.7
Stomach cancer	5.0	1.8
Melanoma	1.6	3.5
Brain cancer	3.1	1.7
Bone and joint cancer	10.0	12.5

[†]"Downwind" here refers to northern Nevada, Utah, and the Arizona Strip.
[††]Columns indicate multiples of the usual rate for each cancer during each time period.
From Richard L. Miller, *Under the Cloud: The Decades of Nuclear Testing*, 384. Reprinted by permission.

FIGURE 3. Downwinder[†] New Cancer Diagnoses Measured During Two Tracking Periods

symptoms. And even then, since the symptoms themselves come on slowly and are easy to confuse with other ailments, diagnosis is notoriously difficult. In its later stages, bone pain and breakage provide clues. Most sufferers do not receive an accurate diagnosis until they are already in stage III, where the median survival time is about three years.

My first traceable symptoms seem to have occurred in May 1993, during my last visit to Japan. I had been experiencing some flu-like symptoms, including fatigue, since arriving in the country two weeks earlier. Then, on a lovely Sunday afternoon, my friend and teaching colleague, Paul Pavich, and I were walking around Lake Yamanaka, one of the five lakes that ring Mt. Fuji. Perhaps half an hour into our walk, I turned white and almost collapsed. The symptom occurred again half an hour later, and Paul and I returned to our hotel. After that the symptoms, though intermittent, included increasing bone pain, particularly in the cervical spine. I attributed the pain to injuries sustained while serving as a Marine, skiing, or hand irrigating my hay field, and assumed that the increasing fatigue was quite reasonably attributable to advancing age. Like many of my gender and generation, I have too often chosen self-diagnosis over seeing a physician.

Within two years of those first symptoms, I found that I did not have sufficient energy to teach a full load at Fort Lewis College and still have strength for much else. Even after taking partial retirement and cutting my teaching load to one semester a year, I still lacked creative energy. I was getting old and there was little to be done, or so I thought.

Accurate diagnosis resulted when I broke two ribs six weeks apart and had unsatisfactory encounters with three different physicians. No one ordered blood tests. The last physician initially failed to take the hard tumor sprouting from my sternum seriously. He dismissed my complaints of steadily worsening pain, particularly in my neck and back, which became worse when I was engaged in his prescribed regimen of physical "therapy."

The root cause of the broken ribs came to light only after I insisted on a CAT scan. On July 5, forty-five years to the day from my exposure at Yucca Flat, I finally received an accurate diagnosis. In addition to the large tumor on my sternum, full body X-rays showed numerous lesions in my head, on my cervical and lumbar spine, and in my ribs, hips, and legs. Such lesions occur when the cancer pushes out from the marrow, eats its way through bone, and leaks contaminated calcium into the bloodstream.

I immediately started oncological radiation, which killed the tumor, and then underwent a standard, three-month course of "front-line" chemotherapy. A few weeks after the series finally ended, a bone aspiration of my hip confirmed that the treatment had failed to reduce the myeloma cells significantly. My best hope was to undergo the arduousness and dangers of a bone stem-cell transplant. Among other unpleasant requirements would be three months in Scottsdale, Arizona, at the Mayo Clinic, including three weeks in a negative-airflow isolation room.

Uh-uh, I thought. No way! It would be far more comfortable to remain at home with Jane and our friends, passively but thankfully surrounded by music, books, and the known. I refused to undergo the transplant.

A week or so later, shortly before Christmas, I sat at my desk struggling to write—something, anything. The depression was getting worse. As if the cancer-related pain, fear, and fatigue were not enough, the side effects of chemotherapy had laid me low. The failure of the regimen slammed me against a dark wall. For months my body had been closing down, collapsing within itself, numb to the sensate world. Despair was sucking me into the void.

Unable to write, I just sat at my desk and stared out the south window. In the background Miles Davis and friends performed the classic tunes of *Kind of Blue*. A few inches of new snow had fallen the night before. The morning sky was a clear, deep, southern Rockies' blue, and calm. Parallel tracks crossed the snow where some fortunate soul had already glided down the street on cross-country skis.

Something touched the edges of my mind. A moment or two later I realized that my shoulders were moving, ever so slightly, to Miles Davis and his trumpet. At first I thought nothing of it and stared down at the few meaningless lines I had scrawled across the page. But when my sore back started to move and my toe picked up the rhythm, the taut lines of my mouth relaxed into a grin. I pushed the page aside and grasped the back of my wheeled office chair, propelling it around the room. After one mad moment and out of breath, I sat back down. A minute or so later I encouraged my body to move. Shoulders moved in syncopated rhythm with each other and with my awakening toes. The splayed fingers of my hands danced along my thighs.

I opened the frosted window and inhaled the scent of blue spruce then restarted *Kind of Blue* and moved my body to a slow and easy series of stretches. I slid into an impromptu version of tai-chi and ended twenty minutes later with a wide open stretch to the heavens. My breath had grown deeper. My passive acceptance and whining anger fell away. I felt tired but committed and newly confident. "No surrender!" I muttered. "Not yet! Not now!" I prayed an old mantra that has often served me well: "Courage! Strength! Courage! Strength!" That afternoon, after conferring with Jane, I called the Mayo Clinic and scheduled a stem-cell transplant.

I have much to be grateful for. Many cancers come on relatively fast, progress rapidly in erratic ways, and kill within months of diagnosis. Many of my fellow atomic veterans died in middle age or even late youth. I am sixty-eight years old and have lived richly, albeit not always wisely. Multiple myeloma didn't really start bothering me until I was in my late fifties and had already spent thirty years pursuing my passion for the classroom, particularly my Shakespeare and writing courses. Unlike many of my fellows, I have lived to see my grandchildren grow up and enter this fractious world. I have enjoyed most of the thirty-five years of living in the mountains and benefited from the love and friendship of good folk. Unlike many of the other atomic veterans and downwinders, I have been blessed with (otherwise) good health and an active, rewarding life.

As a suddenly ill man I am fortunate to have Jane Leonard as my wife, companion, and, more recently, caregiver. This cancer has also turned her life upside down. Caregivers are underappreciated by the outside world. While family, friends, and acquaintances often ask after the well-being of the patient, they seldom ask about the burdens and angst of the caregiver. Her or his fears are at least as profound as those of the patients who are slowly dying. In addition to all else, the caregiver must try to retain some semblance of life apart from the patient and must eventually face life beyond loss. Giving care to a physically failing and ultimately fleeing loved one is a trying vocation. It deserves greater study and greater empathy.

The first month at the Mayo Clinic was spent being interviewed, passing tests, and harvesting stem cells for the eventual transplant. On Valentine's Day, the first day in the isolation room, I received a massive dose of mephalon, the high-dose chemotherapy that we hoped would kill most of the melanoma cells but would definitely destroy my immune system.

On the third day, I received the transplant of stem cells that the technician had "harvested" from my blood two weeks earlier. The concern at that stage of the saga was that they might be unable to harvest sufficient cells for the transplant. To my surprise the technician had extracted far more stem cells than needed, indeed more stem cells than had been harvested from any other man since the transplant clinic had opened three years earlier. I was a clinic celebrity, but only for my gender: the real champ thus far is a woman.

I received a "double dose" of stem cells, the essential seeds for a new immune system. A second such dose sits in the hospital deep freeze. The hope is that a few years down the road I'll still be strong enough to endure the procedure and its side effects.

By the fifth day I knew that, barring infections, I was going to live, albeit with a compromised immune system and permanently fragile bones. It would be a full year until I could receive shots for polio, influenza, pneumonia, and tetanus, and two years before I could receive vaccinations against childhood diseases such as mumps and measles. I would have to avoid close contact with the many babies and small children in my extended family.

Still, life was becoming brighter. For the first time since entering the isolation room I felt how badly I needed to get out of bed and stay out. I had been stretching parts of my body, flexing weak muscles, striving to return from a world of introverted indifference. Late on the morning of the fifth day, I shed my gown. Trailing a portable stand that anchored the various tubes protruding from my body, I limped into the shower and stayed under the spray until my knees weakened. Refreshed and a bit giddy, I turned off the faucet and glanced down at my feet. Water was backing up. What looked like a red toupee blocked the drain. I ran my hand across the top of my head, experienced a moment of shock, and broke into a laugh. I pushed the matted hair away from the drain, sat down on the shower bench, shook my head from side to side and laughed. The high-dose poison was doing its work. No hair means less cancer.

That evening, after a four-hour nap, visits by an assortment of nurses and aides, and my daily visit with Jane, I hobbled toward the large window that looked out on the Sonoran Desert. February and early March were unusually cool and wet in 2002. The blessed rain fell every second or third day. This evening, clouds hung between the far mountains. A couple of hundred yards from my window a large but shallow pool had formed in a bare depression and was lighted by the setting sun. My small section of desert blossomed with many such pools, round and oblong puddles that turned gold in the late light. The backlighted sage glowed a pale translucent green.

Just behind me a La-Z-Boy recliner faced the bed. Feeling a bit faint, I walked around and collapsed into the chair and stared blankly at my cranked-up hospital bed, uneaten dinner, a tray of assorted meds, and the treadmill against the far wall, which I was still too weak to use. "Why am I looking at this horror?" I stood up and slowly turned the recliner 180 degrees so that it faced the window, then sat back down and gazed out across the rain-cleansed desert. Shortly after dusk a coyote approached the pool. After glancing nervously around, he bowed his head and sipped. A moment later something startled him. He sped away, a scrawny gray and beige body almost concealed by a bushy tail.

When I came fully awake the next morning, now twenty-four hours free of morphine, I noticed that someone had turned the La-Z-Boy back around. Once again it faced the bed where I had already spent too much time surrounded by a spider web of medical technology. After eating half of a half-good breakfast and watching what was left of my hair again clog the drain, I hobbled over, turned the chair back toward the window, and plunked down. Two sparrows had landed on the ledge outside my room and were pecking at cracks in the stucco. I gazed at them blankly, somehow caught in another depression.

"Excuse me, sir?" The housekeeper had slipped in to remove my breakfast tray and straighten the room.

"Yes?"

"Sir, are you strong enough to move furniture?"

"I moved it. Twice. Last night someone moved it back. I'd appreciate very much your leaving the chair as it is."

"Yes, sir. No problem. It's just, I've never seen the chair turned around."

Somehow I found that hard to believe, but said, "Thank you for your help." A few minutes later the air-lock door hissed shut behind her.

For the first time in more than a week, I empathized with my fellow patients and their powerfully self-absorbed depression. The housekeeper was probably right. Many patients would not be able to turn the chair. Some may not have thought of it, or even cared. Others could not leave their beds.

Already the pools of the previous evening had mostly drained away and been replaced by green doughnuts of new grass. The indirect light pouring in the window seemed to warm the tears on my face. I had shed more tears in the last few months than at any time since a divorce twenty-four years earlier. But the tears now were not for me. I was crying for the pain this cancer has dealt my loved ones.

After lunch the rains started again, continuing into the early evening. I watched the puddles expand and scanned the desert for life. For a few minutes two cottontails played at the edge of the pool, never straying far from the ocotillo cactus and pale green sage. The rabbits froze then sped back into the brush. A minute later the coyote arrived, sniffed around a bit, then sipped from the pool.

The coyote reminded me of our years on the land. For fourteen years Jane and I had lived a dozen miles south of the La Plata Mountains on seventy-five acres of rolling, irrigated hay field. The open steppe there falls away from the high La Plata peaks and rolls gently to the southwest and the San Juan River. We lived at the northern end of an old-growth piñon and cedar grove and at the bottom of our undulating field, beneath sky and light in constant flux. Along the sunset edge of our field, a strong seasonal stream flowed between a meandering stand of cottonwoods. In the spring I irrigated the field. Olie, our large white mutt, always followed. It was playtime in the Rockies for both of us. In the scrubbed evening light of summer and fall, Jane, Olie, and I walked the perimeter. On winter evenings Olie vainly hunted cottontails while Jane and I carved field-sized figure eights on our skis. At night we sat in front of our aspen- and piñon-fueled stove, listened to music, and pursued our quiet chores. Year after year we watched resident coyotes cross the field and listened to them sing to each other on moonlit nights. We remember the countless times Olie chased coyotes in races he would always lose. He may never have achieved his goal, but Olie was into process.

Another wave of sadness swept over me. That country life was gone, had metamorphosed to memory. Both mind and dreams had bogged down in a foreshortened future. Sitting quietly in the recliner, hands folded over a lap blanket, I stared out the window and tried to let go of my mood. As in a meditation, I watched the night unfold, the clouds thin, and the westward-leaning moon finally sink beyond the far mountains.

Maybe poetry will help, I thought. I opened my poetry bag for the first time since entering the hospital and removed a sheaf of "work in progress." As I read over a few of the poems set at the small farm we called Hawk Dreaming, it struck me that too much mourning would ultimately jaundice the beauty. Instead, I told myself, celebrate that which has been lived. Yes! Three poems particularly helped me across the bridge. They remind me not only of the beauty of life at Hawk Dreaming but also that the world is still rich and fading senses can still sing.

PRESCRIPTION FOR THOSE WINTER BLUES

When the dried air cracks your lips,
the old truck balks in cold dawns,
and the propane man cowers
on the far side of the drifted road;
when the fourth trip this month up
the ice-covered ladder to shovel
the again-groaning roof triggers
yet another black rush of dread:
Don just enough warm clothes, and ski
madly around the glazed field in mile-
long loops. Ski on through the radiance
of late light, as the sun bleeds color

on the far peaks and close, drifted fields.
Feel the rhythm of your pounding breath
as you ski on and on, 'til Venus follows
the lost sun into frozen twilight,
and still on, as Orion strides
across the deepening sky toward spring;
and on through the starred, black night
'til the full moon rises above the snow-
mantled ashes of Burnt Ridge to bathe
the sleeping fields in silver light.

And only then, panting on the raw
edge of exhaustion, turn back
toward that distant flicker of light
that marks both heart and hearth.
As you finally slow your pace, listen!
Blood pounds through head and legs
and throbbing chest. Rejoice in your
deep heart's chant: Life. Life. Life.

❧ ❧ ❧

QUIET TIME

Tonight, as the wind howls across
the fields, I sit empty-minded
before a late solstice fire, content
to file the dull edge of my ditch-
worn spade, its sweat-polished haft

stretched across my lap. While my hands
attend to this rhythmic chore,
the distracted world of Ought
retreats into the howling storm,
like the chaos of an almost-forgotten war.

Jane glides into the room, bends
to kiss my cheek, places a cup
of honeyed tea on the stone hearth,
then pads silently back to the warmth
of her own nest in a far room.
A moment later the taut, haunting
notes of a cello concerto play
chills along my spine. While my aging hands
attend to the tools of spring, I close
my eyes and grin with joy. Like an old hawk
sailing above the orange-streaked fields
of a winter sunset, my smiling heart lifts and sings.

❧ ❧ ❧

A LONG WALK IN THE FIELD AFTER BAD NEWS

Slow down, old friend. Come home.
Listen to the trilling meadowlarks.
Celebrate the magic song of life
Shining in this field at late light.

Succumb to the mood of the pale moon,
Who casts her spell upon the tides,
Bewitching every creature of the sea.

Inhale the piñon-scented breeze of dawn,
When dew sits like hand-strewn pearls
Upon the fading light of autumn leaves.

Relax, my friend. In all these wonders
And a thousand more, life still sings.

By the tenth day I was eating better, walking on the treadmill for ten minutes two or three times a day, and moving beyond the depression that some nights had almost suffocated me. The pools had vanished, replaced by circles of grass where desert birds searched for worms. The shrinking and expanding pools had become far more than a distraction from my introverted room. They reminded me that there are cycles of life and death, that I was a part of that ever-turning wheel, and that it was past time to get on with life.

I rose from my recliner, strode over to the treadmill, and spent the next fifteen minutes walking slowly up a 1 percent grade, possessed by a physical restlessness, an eagerness for action that I had not experienced for many long months. I could hardly wait to get out of the hospital, out of Scottsdale, and back to our home in Durango, back to *Folding Paper Cranes.*

I thought of Sadako Sasaki, the fourteen-year-old Hiba-kusha student who, hoping to survive the ravages of terminal childhood leukemia, attempted to fold one thousand origami cranes. Performing such a feat would bring good luck, accord-ing to tradition. By the time of her death in October 1955, Sadako had been able to fold only 644 cranes, each of which was, in her mind, both a prayer for recovery and a prayer for world peace. Though she was unable to save her own life, her dream of peace lived on. Deeply moved by Sadako's death, her classmates finished folding her cranes, and then continued fold-ing. In the peace parks of Hiroshima and Nagasaki, strings of paper cranes drape memorial after memorial. Sadako Sasaki's prayer for peace has become a world prayer.

After another week my new immune system had taken hold enough to spring me from my prison. Jane had visited every day of my captivity and brought along clean clothes, CDs and DVDs, and edible treats. On liberation day I grinned all the way as she drove me back to our rented apartment. Over the next three weeks she shuttled me to the hospital every other day and sat with me on our sunny terrace or by the swimming pool. At night we sat in front of the TV, glued to CNN and the preemptive, unjustifiable, and tragically miscal-culated war that George W. Bush was unleashing on Iraq, de-spite the advice of wiser people and the disapproval of the rest of the world.

Three weeks later I climbed into the passenger seat and Jane drove us home to our beloved mountains. For most of the drive I rested with my eyes closed. I was leaving a world of almost total dependency and reentering a world of challenges, commitments, and good but demanding work. The descent into and emergence from the transplant had pushed me toward increased clarity and depth of heart, taught me to "let go" of fear and anxiety successfully, and encouraged me to focus instead on the now, the wondrous world of the senses, and this memoir, my attempt to fold words into cranes for peace.

An hour from Durango I finally sat up straight and took an interest in my surroundings. We left the desert behind us and headed north on the La Plata Highway, in home country now, increasing altitude at one hundred feet per mile. The white La Plata peaks scored a clean, deep sky. The trees along the river turned from cottonwoods to cedar and juniper, to piñon and oak, and finally to aspen and ponderosa.

As we entered the house, I glanced around the living room and inhaled familiar smells before I saw something that made me gasp. A five-foot-long assemblage of tiny, brightly colored paper cranes hung from an archway. I was stunned and powerfully moved by the sight. Someone had folded cranes to bring us safely home.

"Look!" As I turned to Jane, who had entered the house behind me, I realized that I was crying. All choked up, I could only repeat the one word. "Look!"

"I know," Jane said, tears in her own eyes. "It was Chyako's idea. She is our hero."

Holding hands we walked up to the rainbow of cranes. Though they were all roughly the same size, perhaps an inch square, and all strung together on monofilament line, each strand and even parts of the same strand had been folded differently, obviously by many hands of varying skill. Almost as if to test the reality of this gift, I touched the cranes and they rustled slightly. Suddenly I felt exhausted by the long drive and overwhelmed by the beauty, compassion, and healing power of the gift before me.

"Chyako organized the foldings. Our friends helped. Even their children folded cranes. Chyako strung the cranes together and our friend Barbara helped her hang them." I found out later that even people we didn't know had folded cranes and added to the power of the collective prayer that had brought us back.

Chyako Hashimoto is a native of Honshu and a former student who has become a good friend, married to a good friend. The two of them have journeyed to Hiroshima and Nagasaki and know the power of hope that paper cranes hold.

Those cranes will stay with me until my death. They symbolize for me the power of collective prayer and loving support, the marvels of modern medicine, and the helping hand of loving kindness and positive thinking. Every day the sight of those beautiful cranes reinforces and deepens my gratitude. My own prayer now is to muster my strength, focus, and discipline to share my journeys to Hiroshima and the International Park for World Peace. In the meantime, I walk in gratitude and sing delight.

part two

The courage to hope

To remember the past is to commit oneself to the future.
To remember Hiroshima is to abhor nuclear war.
To remember Hiroshima is to commit oneself to peace.

— Pope John Paul II

I will write peace on your wings,
and you will fly all over the world.

— Sadako Sasaki, as she folds each crane

The survivor

(Hiroshima, Spring 1981)

For a line of blighted years Fumiko swept
debris from this broken-domed Park for World Peace.
Fumiko-san died today, herself swept away
in the fevered blasts of a long chill.
From the day America's "Little Boy" ravaged
her sweet, mischievous girls, Fumiko seldom spoke
and for too long had grieved alone.
For almost thirty years the survivor swept
the flowered paths, and every day stopped to grieve.
At one gray monument Fumiko stared
at Timiki Hara's keening lament:
> Lost in the shifting sand
>> in the midst of a crumbling world,
>>> the vision of one flower.
But what sustains when that vision fades?
she asked, then closed her weak eyes and fell
once more into the cauldron of time:

8:13: I am already late. My students wait,
Fumiko worries, pink with shame.
Why is this trolley standing still?
My girls! already they sweat at the firebreaks.
The young teacher stares at her open hand,
remembers Akira, dead on Okinawa, remembers
his fingers brushing her quivering palm.
Akira, my love, is dead. A—ki—raaa!
A—ki—raaa! My heart will wither away.
The August sun burns away the light mist.
Above the old trolley, above circling gulls,
one quiet plane scores the cobalt sky; and Man's
blackest magic weaves a howling shroud.

For 10,000 days the silent crone swept
trash from this peaceful park of horrors,
and stopped before each memorial to read
prayers carved from stones of despair:
  As we think of your last moments,
  There are no words.
  We can only weep.
But when no more tears flow? Fumiko
fought another flood tide of memory.
At the Fountain of Prayer she faced words
long since engraved in clawing dreams:
  Dedicated to the souls of those who died
  crying, "Me . . . zu. Me . . . zu." Wa . . . ter.
  Wa . . . ter.

Young Fumiko sprawls in the buckling
street, stares at the crumpled trolley.
Her face and hands bleed. A woman staggers
toward her, naked, glowing. Fleshy sheets
of skin hang from her breasts and shoulders
like the crimson folds of a leather chemise.
She holds a dead, blackened girl, whose blistered
mouth is locked in one long howl.

Fumiko stands to fight through crowds
of moaning dead. "My girls! My girls! My girls!"
she screams, as terror pulls her deeper into hell,
"Me . . . zu," the last girls cry. "Me . . . zu.
   Me . . . zu . . . "
All is changed now, woefully changed
The world has blown away.

As one cursed to live apart, Fumiko dropped
to a stone bench. A line of bowing pilgrims
paused before the Cenotaph to read a stark pledge:
   May all those souls buried here rest
   in peace; for we shall not repeat the evil.

Old Fumiko shook her wrinkled head.
But what of all the ever-yearning lost,
their empty souls adrift in the wind?

Young Fumiko finds her girls, a broken line
of charred sticks, their dresses smoldering,
their eyes raw, simmering pits.
"Aieeeee... My girls! My girls!" She screams
at the black sky, "Emiko... Meiko... Ukiko... "
Keening name after name, she counts
and straightens bundles of charred rags,
and then hears one shrill moan: "Me... zu... "
Fumiko extends her trembling hand to touch
the cracked lips of one still-living girl.
"Aiii... eeeeee! Uuuu... kiii... ko... "
The breathing ghost moans, "Me... zu. Me... "
and fades away. Ukiko too has changed.
A little world has blown away.

But today, in this lovely park that prays
for peace, cherry blossoms scent the air,
and lines of children drape monuments of bronze
and stone with bright garlands of paper cranes.
Old Fumiko stopped before a stone cube
and gazed once more at Sankochi Toge's plea:
Give me my sons and daughters back.
Give me back myself.
Give back the human race
As long as this life lasts, this life,
Give back peace that will never end.

No, she moans. All is changed, forever changed.
All that we love has burned away.

The old teacher glanced up, startled
by a pigtailed girl dancing on wet rocks
that line the river bank. The smiling girl waved,
then, like an autumn leaf, quivered and fell away.
"My girls! My girls!" Fumiko tried to scream,
her long-mute voice a croak of rust.
Waving stick-thin arms, the lost teacher
hobbled toward the deep, black stream,
as puzzled pilgrims slowly stopped to stare.

"Uki... " Fumiko croaked, then leaped. "Uki... ko!"
Moments later, rescued, she held the girl
close against her wet, shaking breast.
Rocking back and forth, the teacher cooed, "Uki... ko,
Uki... ko," until the frightened child scurried free.
"My girls! My girls!" the haunted woman moaned,
as the small crowd bowed deeply and thinned away.
Hands reached out to the mumbling crone.
"Come now, Grandmother. Please, come with us.
You are wet. You will chill and sicken."
But lost in years of ash, Fumiko fails to hear.
My girls, my love, the world, all has changed,
changed finally. Our future has blown away.

Again and again she keened her hoarse refrain:
"Uki...ko
   Uk...i...ko
     U...ki..."

A flight of cranes

In *Hiroshima* John Hersey records in stunningly effective language the specific agonies of August 6, 1945 and shortly thereafter, when peace existed only in the charred and blistered silence of the dead. That is the image of Hiroshima most of us carry: a nuclear wasteland where the future will never dawn. Fortunately for the rest of the world, Hiroshima's history did not end with its obliteration.

The heart of modern Hiroshima is its International Park for World Peace. On Hiroshima Day 1952, after almost seven years of great sacrifice on the part of the Hibakusha, the Park for World Peace opened its arms to a fractious world. During the arduous process of financing and building their Peace Park, the survivors also created a World Federalist City committed to what they perceive to be a holy, essential, and interdependent trinity: world brotherhood, world peace, and nuclear disarmament. In the process of re-creating themselves, the Hibakusha have both memorialized and transcended their nuclear apocalypse.

Perhaps more than any other place on earth, Hiroshima and its Peace Park personify the phoenix, consumed by flames and horror only to rise from its ashes transformed and radiant. The park is more than a place to mourn the dead and confront the horrors of our darkest potential. Here the attentive pilgrim can also discern and grasp tenuous threads of hope. We have the capacity to grow wiser. The question is, do we possess the will?

When I first visited the Peace Park in 1954, I failed to grasp its premise or see its vision. I was a high school dropout, an eighteen-year-old Marine dragged along to Hiroshima by an older and wiser buddy. Not until the months following my own nuclear apotheosis at Yucca Flat three years later did I even begin to glimpse the import of what I had encountered in Hiroshima.

In June of 1981, twenty-four years after Yucca Flat and Shot Hood, I finally made my first trip back, accompanied by Jane. From that visit I developed great respect for the Peace Park and its vision. Sad to say, however, that respect was more than balanced by my own despair and a deeply etched fear of approaching nuclear Armageddon. Not until 1993 and my third visit did I fully grasp the Hibakusha's vision and feel their tenuous but abiding hope.

❧ ❧ ❧

Like a hard spring that starts as winter dregs but finally buds to light, that last pilgrimage ended well, far better than it began. For the first two days of the visit I wandered through intermittent rain to scores of stone memorials, most of which whispered grief. I felt little but despair and cynicism. Toward the end of the second day, however, the sun burned away the dark clouds and, in a variety of ways, I found what I needed.

When I left Yokohama for the final stage of a long journey, I had been in Japan for little more than a day, was still jet-lagged, and seemed to suffer from one of the many viruses that thrive in the stale air of long flights. I had risen at dawn that May morning and traveled for more than an hour on two different local trains in order to catch the bullet train south at 8:33. Sick, depressed, and surrounded by rows of silent, conservatively dressed passengers and a thickening shroud of loneliness, I spent the last four hours of the trip heading south-southwest through a steady downpour.

May 1993 began unusually wet. After three days of heavy rain, freshly plowed fields had collapsed to muck. Torn branches and blowing ribbons of leaves, blossoms, and trash littered the fields and streets and backed up in overflowing gutters. In the towns we whizzed past, the few shoppers crouched under umbrellas and scurried across windblown streets. As the train sped by a wide expanse of flooded rice fields, an image carried me back to my reluctant 1954 journey. On that muggy July day three Marines had ridden south on a rickety, nineteenth-century train that bucked and shook the entire distance. Today, as then, partially protected from sun and rain by conical straw hats, farm women bent over the rice. As quickly as the memory appeared, it receded into an almost-forgotten past.

At Mishima Station, the bullet train's first stop, a dozen passengers rose from their seats, hunched their shoulders fur-

ther into defensive space and shuffled down the aisle to the
vestibule, where they donned raincoats and prepped black
umbrellas. As the train slowed, they faced outward, heads
bent, faces fixed impassively against the downpour. Well
before the last passenger had stepped down, new arrivals
pushed silently into the vestibule. In the process of closing umbrellas and doffing rain gear, the new arrivals whispered
apologies to each other. Mostly gray-headed, they entered the
car singly, each bowing slightly to those already seated, before
gliding unobtrusively to the best available seat. The seat next
to me remained empty.

The last person to enter was a badly bent woman who
walked with a cane. Rain dripped down her tightly woven bun
of white hair and her mask of deep wrinkles. The old woman
glanced at the seat next to me and crept on down the aisle only
to return, bow stiffly, and seat herself just as the train pulled
from the station. When I bowed back and smiled, she turned
away and sat slightly forward, her blotched, beige and white
hands folded in her lap, her unwavering eyes focused on the seat
in front. I shivered, huddled within my raincoat, and moved
closer to the window. At the next stop she changed seats.

I gazed through the rain-streaked glass and tried to sort
out my confusion about the trip. A few weeks earlier when I'd
told friends I was heading back to Hiroshima, one asked:
"You've already been there twice, Red. What's the big need?"
Jane reminded me of the quiet despair I had brought back
from my 1981 visit. Another friend put on her bemused face:
"We all know about the *bomb,* Red. And we know what

happened to you on the Nevada desert. But seriously, it's so far back. Don't you think maybe it's time to move on?"

"Perhaps," I remember saying. Perhaps, but not quite yet. How does one just set aside events that have determined so much of one's life? However confused and self-indulgent the journey seemed to some of my friends and, at times, even to myself, I knew that it was a pilgrimage I had to make, and that I had to make it alone. I badly needed, finally, to weave together the disparate threads of my history with Hiroshima and Yucca Flat.

Even though it was the first Friday in May and the start of Golden Week, Japan's always-anticipated four-day weekend, the towns we sped through seemed deserted—a few cars sneaking through puddle after puddle, a few desperate souls dashing through the torrents with umbrellas, a biker, head down as if well launched on the Tour de France, the wings of his yellow slicker flapping to hold him back.

As the only foreigner in the car, if not on the entire train, I felt like what I was, a not-quite-invisible alien lost on an unfriendly island; an eccentric American traveling to Hiroshima to sort out the hopes, fears, and delusions of a confused life. Save for the soft, lulling *whiiishhhh* of the bullet train on its seamless tracks, I had dropped into a movie without a sound track. Only once did someone acknowledge my presence. At Osaka a thin but ramrod-erect man wearing a brown suit and carrying a tan raincoat took the seat across the aisle. He turned my way and stared through thick, tortoise-shell glasses. When I attempted a feeble smile, he smiled tightly, gave a curt bow of the head, and faced forward.

As the train turned westward, my anxiety increased. We were crossing the low, green mountains that shelter Hiroshima from most storms—most, but not all. Forty-eight years earlier these same mountains had intensified the destruction wrought by Little Boy. When the bomb exploded over the large, fan-shaped delta upon which Hiroshima is built, the surrounding mountains first contained the nuclear tsunami then bounced it back over the city like a boomerang. The first blast all but flattened the city; the boomerang destroyed most of what had been left standing and ignited the fires that consumed the city and most of its inhabitants.

Hiroshima's natural amenities have contributed greatly to its old (and new) prosperity, as well as to its destruction. From the crescent of low mountains, the Ota River flows into its delta, divides into seven estuaries, and empties into Ujina Harbor, one of Japan's most important. From the very beginning of the Pacific War in the early 1930s, Ujina Harbor was the major point of embarkation for troops and supplies headed for Manchuria, Korea, and China. Because of the harbor's strategic location in the narrow strait between Honshu and Kyushu, Hiroshima became the second most important military center in Japan. In the final year of the war, the city was the hub of the effort to defend against the Allied invasion of Kyushu, expected in November 1945. Despite its military importance, however, Hiroshima remained one of the very few major Japanese cities to escape firebombing. To American strategists, who desired the most traumatic impact possible, Hiroshima presented a perfect target for Little Boy.

Hiroshima's geography, a flat delta surrounded by sea and mountains, ensured almost total destruction.

❧ ❧ ❧

A few minutes after crossing the mountains, the train glided to a stop at Hiroshima Central Station, two kilometers from ground zero, yet almost totally destroyed in the blast and its fiery aftermath. When I first came this way in 1954, the huge, ruined station seemed to be nothing more than a barren wilderness of congested tracks. The few civilians aboard that slow, bone-rattling train wore threadbare, prewar clothes or parts of their military uniforms. Today wider tracks and bullet trains whisk full cars of well-dressed Japanese around the perimeter of Honshu. Today at Central Station green canvas canopies shade dozens of long, elevated platforms, each of which sports rows of vending machines, green metal benches, and potted, flowering trees, all in full blossom.

Besides its harbor and Peace Park, the city is best known for its cut-flower industry and for its annual flower festival. As I would discover, the flower festival, the celebration of spring, Children's Week, and the Peace Park have all become as inextricably entwined as tightly knit threads. It is finally through the magic of this tapestry that Hiroshima is best understood. Contrary to the American image of the city, Hiroshima not only mourns its catastrophe but, more importantly, like the new and brilliant phoenix that it has become, the City of Flowers celebrates new life.

As I rose to follow my fellow passengers into the great tunnels and caverns of Hiroshima Central, I felt a shivering chill of recognition. However these gray fellow passengers and I might differ, I was of their generation and, in my own hapless way, a distant cousin to their experience. In 1945 most of those now disembarking from the train would have been children, teenagers, young adults. Many of the boys who were fourteen or older at the time would have been soldiers. At least in my imagination, my traveling companions were the Hibakusha. Their return to this city, like my own, was at least one part pilgrimage.

I walked down the platform stairs and pushed into the throngs pouring into the tunnel, where silent but assertive bodies competed for vanishing space in the rapidly clotting crowd. Almost immediately I found myself hyperventilating, my lungs again constricted by the claustrophobia I had first experienced as a young Marine cringing at the bottom of a dark trench. I pushed my way to the side of the crowd and stood in a small alcove long enough to pull out my asthma inhalator, take a couple of deep hits, and breathe deeply for a moment or two. Twenty minutes later, after the crowd had thinned, and after struggling through a few hundred meters of platforms, tunnels, and two-story-high waiting rooms, I pushed through the main entrance and into the open air. Across the station square, through the scrim of a light shower and less than a hundred yards away, the green neon sign of my hotel blinked a misleading invitation. I leaned against a wall, breathed deeply for a moment, and then dragged my aching body across the rain-shimmering square.

Aware that it was still hard for Americans to get rooms in Hiroshima, I had asked my friend Tsuyoshi Ogura, manager of

the International Education System, to make the reservation,
which the desk clerk now did not want to honor. The absolute
model of deference, the clerk smiled, nodded, and said, "I am
so sorry, sir. We believe Westerners will find our facilities not
adequate."

I knew it was rude to stay where I wasn't wanted, but
didn't care. With a confirmed reservation I was not about to
trot off half-sick into the rain. Trying to maintain both my
own smile and the deep, authoritarian tone of the Marine sergeant I had once been, I fought to counter the clerk's obsidian
eyes, alabaster smile, and hypocritical solicitude. After a long
minute or two, face flushed but dazzling smile still frozen in
place, the clerk slapped hotel and police registration forms on
the counter and failed to offer me a pen.

Once in my tiny but well-appointed room on the third
floor, I glanced out the window. The rain had again intensified
and now shot straight down into multiplying and converging
puddles that looked to swallow the street. I drew a hot bath in
the deep, square tub and prepared to unwind. The trip from
Durango to this bath had consumed four days: a half-day
drive to Albuquerque, a flight to Los Angeles, another half day
of boredom waiting for the evening departure to Tokyo, a day
in Yokohama making arrangements, and the early-morning
departure to Hiroshima. As badly as I wanted to get to the
Peace Park, I needed to rest and, if possible, wait out the rain.

An hour later I sat at the small desk next to my narrow bed
and stared out across the shimmering asphalt square. The
great concave facade of Hiroshima Central and its thick con-

crete pillars hovered like a bad dream. I remembered Kildare
Dobbs's story of fifteen-year-old Emiko, who happened to be
standing behind one of the pillars when Little Boy detonated
and who survived the blast. Like so many thousands of other
students who had been evacuated to surrounding villages,
every day Emiko and her little sister rode the train into the city
to help build firebreaks, a dirty, grueling task assigned to girls,
the old, and the militarily unfit. Emiko arrived at Hiroshima
Central shortly before Little Boy detonated six hundred
meters above Shima Hospital. Even at a distance of two kilometers, had Emiko not been standing behind one of the station's massive pillars, she would most certainly have died.
Weakened by injury and traumatized by the surrounding
horror, Emiko managed to join the lines of temporary survivors struggling toward the foothills. Hours later she arrived
at a rural train station and finally found her way home. Only
later did Emiko learn that her sister and most of their friends
had perished.[20]

As I gazed out at the huge pillars behind which little Emiko
had once stood, the memory of her story fed the depression
that had led me back to Hiroshima. Now, hunched over the
desk, I tried to sort out a small slice of the past. Reasons for
this pilgrimage had been evolving ever since my descent into
the irradiated trenches of Yucca Flat thirty-six years earlier.
However, it was not shivering at the bottom of a five-foot-
deep trench that brought me back here. Nor was it the earth-
shattering roar of the blast and shock waves that had passed
two feet above where I crouched. Nor the forty-thousand-foot

high mushroom that had risen from ground zero to blot out the predawn stars. Like the Angel of Death in the Land of Goshen, both the blast and the shock wave passed harmlessly overhead. The mushroom struck me even then as an awesome symbol—but only a symbol, not something personally and immediately relevant. What muted my life and turned me ever so slowly back to Hiroshima was the forced march, just a few hours after detonation, to ground zero, with its swirling winds and radioactive dust.

My horror of that dust did not begin until the spring of 1958. As a brand-new college student and family man not quite getting by on the Korean G.I. Bill, I finally devoured John Hersey's *Hiroshima,* which, a few years earlier, my buddy Begay had encouraged me to read. Hersey's stunning narrative seemed to trip a delayed switch. Within days of finishing it, I experienced a long series of recurring nightmares in which three unborn children died. Even then consciousness dawned slowly, as small but important changes poisoned my body.

Thyroid disease was the first announcement, coming sometime in 1960. I started passing out when I stood still for more than a few moments or when I bent over to tie my shoes. At first I joked about the problem, which I attributed to carrying a full academic load at college, working forty hours a week, and getting no exercise. My doctor took the problem more seriously.

Over the years there have been other announcements, all bad. And over the years I have learned a lot about the downwinders and about the hundreds of thousands of nuclear veterans, many of whom, like myself, suffer from various cancers at a rate far higher than others of our generation, but whose complaints the government chose for many years to ignore.

Not until 1962 did I fully grasp what was happening to me and, I began to imagine, to many of my comrades who had made that unjustified march to and from ground zero. Other than the thyroid problem, which I did not then connect to radiation disease and which I was successfully medicating, all seemed well. The first few years after Shot Hood saw the end of the Eisenhower era, and the national nightmare that ended Camelot. Despite the turmoil in the black ghettos, rumors from another Asian war, and the assassinations that were to rock our smug complacency, life seemed rich, for me and for increasing numbers of others. As had so many of our fathers, uncles, and older brothers from World War II, we veterans abandoned working-class jobs and poured into colleges and universities on our Korean G.I. bills. Jobs were usually plentiful, housing was relatively cheap, and the fulfillment of the American dream beckoned from what seemed to be an ever-nearing horizon. Though my thoughts often returned to Yucca Flat and Hiroshima, and though the two had already merged in my occasional nightmares, I was a happy young man.

Seven months after inhaling the seventy-four-kiloton assault that was Shot Hood, I left the Marines to enter college, from which I graduated a few weeks after John F. Kennedy made his wonderfully inspiring call: "Ask not what your country can do for you. Ask rather what you can do for your country." By the summer of 1962 I was well launched in graduate studies. I enjoyed a well-paying fellowship, a supportive wife, and a five-year-old son who had been born shortly before I descended into the trenches of Yucca Flat. Life was good. All we were missing was a few more children.

After spending many months failing to conceive, my wife visited a gynecologist. We both assumed the problem was hers. Barbara returned from her examination with good news. She was fertile and absolutely healthy. With a puzzled frown on her face, she asked me to visit her doctor and submit to a test. A week later I peered through a microscope at a Petri dish in which a few hundred sperm cells squirmed listlessly.

"There should be thousands of those little critters," the doctor said. "And they should be a helluva lot more active." Later in his office he added, "I'm sorry, Mr. Bird, but the chances of you fathering another child are quite remote." After peering for a moment at my shocked but silent reaction, the doctor added, "And if you did by chance succeed, well... there exists a considerably heightened risk for deformity." Though no longer a believer, I am part of a large, close Mormon family. Barbara had four sisters. We wanted at least two or three siblings for our small son. I felt like a door had been slammed in my face. That doctor was the first person to suggest a connection between my thyroid condition, sterility, ionizing radiation, and Shot Hood.

Later that afternoon, my eyes welling with tears, I sat on the couch with my arm around Barbara and told her that we were not to have the large family we so badly wanted. After a shocked gasp, a long wail rose from deep inside her. She dou-

bled over, as if jolted by a stomach spasm. I took her in my arms
and tried my best to extend comfort and reassurance that I was
far from feeling. "I'm sorry," I mumbled impotently, repeating
myself until too choked to go on. Our son, David, sat beside us
and held on to his mother. Though he did not understand why
his parents were upset, he too was crying. I reached around to
embrace both of them and said, "At least God has given us our
David." Though our gratitude was real and deep, so was our
disappointment and our heart-emptying sense of irretrievable
loss. In the following months I again felt an increasingly strong
need to return to Hiroshima, though another eighteen years
were to pass before I made my way back.

≋   ≋   ≋

I shook my head and tried to pull my mind from the past. Rain
or no, I had spent too much time, money, and energy on this
journey to lose myself in self-pity. After staring sightlessly for
a while longer at the incessant rain, I washed my face with
cold water, donned my rain gear, and headed for the Peace
Park. For ten minutes I stood under the small canvas portico
of the Green Hotel, then dashed through the rain toward the
arriving east–west trolley, which reverses directions at Hiroshima Central. I would get off at the Aioi Bridge, ten stops and
fifteen minutes distant. As it did in August 1945, the trolley
loops to the east and south before heading west, where it passes
through the center of the city at ground zero, within fifty meters
of the park's north entrance. It occurred to me that my entire
stay in Hiroshima would be within the four-thousand-meter
diameter of total devastation.

The trolley left the station with few passengers: myself and a trio of old women, each of whom wore a black raincoat and carted a large handbag and small cardboard suitcase. Though most older Japanese avert their eyes when approaching strangers, all three women stared at me and frowned. The trolley filled quickly. After the third stop the only seats left were, once again, the ones closest to me.

At the fifth stop, three teenage girls in blue and white school dresses took one look at me, giggled, grabbed the vacant bench opposite, and immediately launched into a whispered conversation. One of the girls turned to me, eyes wide and smile somewhat tremulous. "Good-a aftanoon, sir."

"Good afternoon, Miss." The other girls stared at me, intrigued. My smile triggered the first smiles I had received that day.

The speaker's face glowed. Touching her fingertips first to her chest and then to her forehead, she said, "I Meiko." She looked straight into my eyes, which struck me as mischievous, as if she took neither herself nor me seriously. "You are Amelican, yes?" Her friends laughed and turned away, titillated by Meiko's rudeness.

"Yes, Meiko, I am an American." I smiled again.

"Prease, you teach-a me Engrish?" Immediately her friends turned back toward us.

"*Hai, hai.* Plactise Engrish," the others pleaded.

From the back of the trolley a woman hissed something to the effect of "shut-up and mind your manners!" The three girls changed to prim mannequins. The joy left their faces and they drew away. I turned my head to see who had punctured the mood. One of the trio of old women glared back, her mouth set as a taut wire, her narrow eyes unwavering.

I dropped my gaze and turned back toward the girls. Though they sat with backs erect and hands folded demurely in their laps, they could not quite manage to suppress their giggles. A few minutes later Meiko turned and whispered, "Sir? You go Peace-u Park-u?"

"Excuse me, Meiko?"

"Sir, you go Peace-u Park-u, *ne?*"

"Yes, thank you."

"Oh!" she frowned. "We can-a no mo plactise." She reached up and pulled the cord to alert the conductor. "Peace-u Park-u," Meiko said, pointing across the street, obviously disappointed.

I rose, took a step or two down the aisle, and turned back to the girls. "I am sorry to go. Thank you for your smiles." Relieved that the rain had stopped at least for the moment, I stepped from the trolley and cut across the boulevard toward the northern entrance.

Roughly two hundred meters wide at its southern end, which borders Grand Peace Boulevard, the park narrows like an arrowhead as it stretches north-northwest. The five-hundred-meter-long arrowhead occupies a peninsula formed by the gradually diverging Hon and Motoyasu Rivers. The site includes ground zero. At 8:16 a.m. on August 6, 1945, the temperature at the hypocenter exceeded six thousand degrees centigrade.[21]

In their terrified attempts to escape the fires that burned all around them, many of the survivors headed for the rivers and canals. In central Hiroshima, most of those who made it boiled in the superheated waters. Of those few hundred who reached the peninsula where the park now stands, almost all either died shortly or drowned in the unusually high tide that swept up the estuaries from the Inland Sea on that black and orange evening. By the following morning the rivers were so gorged with swollen bodies that it was difficult to see the water. Like the rivers, the peninsula was covered with hundreds of already-bloating corpses.[22]

The small peninsula is part of the prewar neighborhood of Zaimoku-cho. There on August 6, some four hundred meters southwest of ground zero, 540 thirteen- and fourteen-year-old girls labored to tear down buildings and clear away the debris to form firebreaks. Throughout the country, clearing lanes to contain fires had become the primary mission of civil defense. Like Emiko and so many other thousands of children who had been evacuated from the city to outlying villages, the girls of Zaimoku-cho entrained daily to their assigned work details. Hiroshima's citizens were preparing for what they thought would be the worst. As the second most important military center in Japan, Hiroshima expected the same kind of fire-bombing that by the summer of 1945 had destroyed huge areas of Tokyo, Yokohama, Osaka, Kobe, and dozens of other Japanese cities.

At the firebreaks of Zaimoku-cho, most of the girls died instantly or were critically wounded. Some made their way to the Motoyasu River, where they leaped into the boiling water. An Army search party rescued a few others. All died in the coming days.[23]

Today the peninsula has metamorphosed into the International Park for World Peace, a lush refuge of open lawns and shady groves where flowers bloom and thousands of white doves nest. Peace is present, palpable. However, as one moves through the park, from one granite memorial to another, and to the next and the next, the apparent serenity takes on texture and resonance. The strong counterpoint to fecund and orchestrated serenity is inescapable and orchestrated confrontation—with the past, with the Hibakusha, with the politics of fear, and with our ancient and tragic need to see most of our species as "other" and hence "lesser."

At first encounter the dark memorials obscure any more hopeful note. As I was to rediscover over the next two days, however, the once corpse-strewn peninsula has become far more than the world's most infamous tomb. Yes, pilgrims journey here both to mourn and be confronted, as well we should. But we also come to celebrate the sometimes-great human consciousness. The park's most priceless gift? A shrine toward which lost pilgrims might well journey in quest of hope.

Vision and hope are the intertwined strands that rebuilt and transformed Hiroshima. As we all realize, hope glimmers as the most elusive, fragile, and essential of emotions. Without vision, hope fades; without hope, vision dies. More than any other propelling motivation, it was hope, a vision of what the world *could* become, and almost unbelievable self-discipline,

...built and transformed Hiroshima. And more than all else, it was my own confused and tangled pursuit of hope that had drawn me back to this bustling modern city and its beautiful, darkly yet vibrantly sacred Park for World Peace.

The park seemed almost deserted, perhaps because of the rain, perhaps because it was the Friday before Golden Week. The few people scurrying along the paths, heads bent under their umbrellas, seemed to be using the park more as a convenient shortcut than as a destination. Lonely and out-of-place, I stood beneath a sheltering tree and stared across the Motoyasu River at the four-story-tall ruin now known as the A-bomb Dome, the world's most recognized symbol of nuclear destruction. Despite its proximity to the hypocenter, several walls of the brick-and-steel building survived the blast, including the steel girders of the central dome. After the blast and fires that leveled most of the city, the domed ruin stood as the most prominent skeleton within a two-kilometer radius. Though the rain recommenced as a light drizzle, I sat on a green metal bench, stared at the huge gray boulders along the riverbank, and thought of the young girls I had met on the trolley, particularly Meiko and her pleasing boldness. I relished their youth, innocence, and silliness, and mourned their vulnerability.

Lost again in musing about my own nuclear inheritance, I rose from the bench. Though I felt like turning back to my hotel and a yearned-for cocoon of warm blankets, I followed my slanting umbrella past a number of memorials I hoped later to revisit and headed for the Children's Peace Memorial, best known as the Tower of a Thousand Cranes. Along the way I tiptoed through a large circle of tame white doves, the descendants of those two hundred doves released forty years earlier to symbolize a profound hope: "No more Hiroshimas."[24]

The Tower of a Thousand Cranes is but one of many memorials that eulogize the roughly six thousand students, mostly girls, killed by America's Little Boy. Several of these memorials speak of the relationship between sacrifice and peace. Atop the Mobilized Students' Merciful Kannon, for example, stands a statue of Kannon, the Buddhist goddess of peace, whose arms stretch open in a gesture of acceptance. Engraved on the base, a poem by Yasuo Yamamoto reads: "In reverence of the spirits of these students / Who have become Kannons preserving peace."[25]

Another memorial eulogizes the 350 victims from the Hiroshima Second Middle School and states that the dead girls have "become the cornerstone of peace." The hope is the same: may their deaths provide the requisite sacrifice. Though the most optimistic epigraphs dare to suggest hope, others, perhaps more realistically, cry a more haunting sentiment: "As we think of your last moments / there are no words. We can only weep."

Of those several memorials whose effects have resonated within me the longest and are probably most responsible for pulling me back to this beautiful burial ground, one of the most central is the Tower of a Thousand Cranes. Despite the angst I carried home from my journey here twelve years earlier, the tower did more to nurture a slender reed of hope than did any other aspect of the journey. Why? Because of what this memorial has wrought. I returned hoping the miracle would recur.

In 1955 when fourteen-year-old Sadako Sasaki's death from radiation sickness halted her crane making, her class-mates took up the task. Though Sadako's courage and faith failed to save her, the dying girl's determination transformed countless others. Shortly after her death Sadako's sorrowful classmates launched a movement to build a memorial to comfort her soul and to express their own fragile hopes for world peace. These young students inspired a Japan-wide campaign that resulted in the Children's Monument.[26]

Under the protection of a nine-meter-tall, three-legged, bronze cone stands the statue of a young boy and girl, who represent new hope. Atop the sheltering cone stands a statue of Sadako Sasaki in her school uniform, her arms extended upward, hands holding a golden crane. The monument bears two inscriptions: "Peace on the Earth and in the Heavens" and "This is our cry. This is our prayer. For building Peace in this world." The prayer, crowned by a symbol of hope, epitomizes the park's most profound yet subtlest theme.

Throughout Japan, Peace Studies is a core part of the cur-riculum. As ongoing horrors in the rest of the world continu-ously attest, we are what we're taught. The Tower of a Thou-sand Cranes teaches well. Since its unveiling on Children's Day, May 5, 1958, Sadako's memorial has become a magnet for schoolchildren from throughout Japan and has inspired children-oriented peace projects around the world.[27]

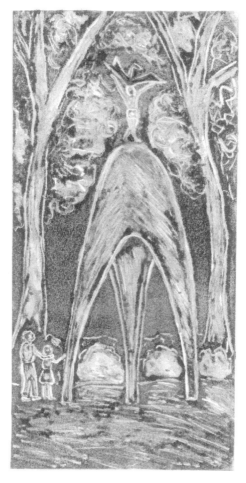

FIGURE 4. Tower of a Thousand Cranes, Children's Peace Memorial, International Park for World Peace, Hiroshima. Monoprint by Jane Leonard.

When Jane and I journeyed here in June 1981, we sat on a bench across from the tower and watched as scores of students descended from their yellow school buses to enter the park. Most carried brightly colored strings of cranes. Their first stop was Sadako's memorial. Each group formed a line and waited patiently. Slowly, reverently, student after student stepped forward, bowed his or her young head in prayer, draped one more string of colored cranes over countless predecessors, and stepped back to pray again. Jane and I returned to this spot several times during our visit, each time more moved by the simple faith of Japan's schoolchildren.

Today, however, the park seemed devoid of children, and the three days of heavy rain had washed away much of the color. Like Buddhist prayer flags after too much time in the elements, the rain-bleached cranes had already given up their prayers. Bled-out dyes formed multicolored puddles around the statue's bronze feet, as if commenting upon both Sadako's vain effort and the innocent hopes of Japan's children. That the paper cranes ultimately fade is wonderfully irrelevant to the children who place them here, however. As long as our world manages to endure, children will continue to come here, quietly await their turns, then add their strings of cranes and their prayers to this simply elegant altar to peace.

I pulled my thoughts away from the Children's Peace Memorial and headed across the park to the Atomic Memorial Mound. In the days and weeks following the holocaust, squads of rescuers cremated the remains of some ninety thousand initial victims. Eventually relatives received the ashes of those who could be identified. In 1955 the city built a sanctuary for the ashes of the unidentified dead. On top of a large, domed mound of grass stands an ivory statue of Kannon. Beneath the mound lie the ashes of those thousands of victims who remain anonymous—though not unmourned. At this spot on August 6 each year the Hiroshima Religious Federation offers a memorial service for these nameless victims.

For the first time since entering the park I encountered fellow pilgrims. A very old man and woman stood before the Atomic Mound with their heads bowed. Both were short and thin, but the woman was tiny, hunchbacked, and not much more than four feet tall. Both wore long black raincoats and stood under a single black umbrella. A few feet away, also under an umbrella, stood a man in a tan raincoat who seemed vaguely familiar.

FIGURE 5. Atomic Memorial Mound, International Park for World Peace, Hiroshima. Monoprint by Jane Leonard.

I faced the site and bowed my head in respect. Almost immediately, a thin but intense voice pierced the silence. I turned my head to confront the angry eyes of the old woman, who was pointing at me and repeating a question in Japanese. The only word I understood was, "'Melican," American. Her husband tried to get her to stop pointing at me, but she ignored him.

"*Gomannasai,*" I ventured, bowing very low. "I am very sorry. *Gomannasai, Oto-san.*" I have seldom felt so completely out of place. Who the hell did I think I was? And what did I presume? Though my mind told me to walk away as rapidly as possible, I stood rooted in place, frozen by embarrassment.

After a long minute the man in the tan raincoat stepped forward, smiling effusively. "Excuse me if I am out of my place, sir." He bowed slightly to me and more deeply toward the old couple. "This lady think you American. She want to know, how can you be so shameless as come this place?"

"I don't know," I mumbled. "I believe in peace..." When I paused the man started to turn toward the old couple. I held up my hand to stop him. "Please," I continued. "I also came to spend some time thinking, and seeking...something. *Gomannasai, dozo?* I am sorry to have intruded here." Starting and ending with the little old woman, I bowed deeply to each of the three.

The smiling man turned toward the couple and translated. Though the hostility seemed to drop from her tone, the old woman shook her head and muttered something back. "I am sorry," the translator said. "You can not know what we know. You can not feel what we feel."

"No...no," I stammered. "I can't." I needed to explain my kinship with this place and its importance in my life, but tears came to my eyes and I could not shape my feelings into words. Mumbling, "Sorry, so sorry," I turned hastily away, crossed to the east side of the park, and almost stumbled across Motoyasu Bridge and into the Han Dori Mall. The busy mall, which rose literally from ground zero, is a two-block-long covered street full of fancy shops, souvenir stands, and restaurants.

In a moment of déjà vu, it was 1954 again and I was feeling for the first time the acute loneliness that often comes from venturing into countries, cultures, and neighborhoods where an American is too often an unwelcome reminder of past horrors. At the first pay phone, disregarding the expense and forgetting that it was the middle of the night in Colorado, I called Jane collect to tell her how much I loved and missed her, and to hear her reassuring words. After the call, somewhat stronger but still depressed, I walked down the mall to the Sweden Bakery, a two-story coffee shop that has, since Jane and I ate there in 1981, evolved into a first-rate and always crowded cafeteria.

Surrounded by the warmth and the voices of customers and waitresses, I sat down with a large mug of hot chocolate and wrapped an invisible blanket around myself. After a couple of long sips I placed my cold hands around the mug and drifted back to my second journey here, twelve years earlier.

In 1981 I had a chance to spend May teaching in Japan. Through the good offices of my friend Jim Ash, who knew how badly I wanted to revisit Hiroshima, I was able to obtain a position with the International Education System (IES) in Tokyo. Shigemitso Ogura, the founder of IES, and his son Tsuyoshi believed that education exchanges between Japan and America would foster human understanding and mutual appreciation and would contribute to world peace. It was my job to help polish students' English skills and prepare them for success in American colleges. At the end of my teaching assignment, Jane flew over and accompanied me on my pilgrimage to three spots: Mt. Fuji, where I had been stationed in the Marines; Kyoto, the cultural center of Japan; and Hiroshima. Jane appreciated my reasons for wanting to visit the first two sites but could not initially understand my need to return to Hiroshima. By the time we left, however, she shared both my angst and my commitment.

By 1981 much had changed. Japan had become the economic miracle of the world, and Hiroshima was no longer the sea of shacks punctuated by a few steel-and-concrete ruins that I had so reluctantly visited in 1954. The city had risen from its ashes to become a symbol of highly prosperous Japanese modernity. New skyscrapers and beautiful residential areas had replaced the shanties. Well-dressed businessmen, fashionable women, and traffic jams had replaced the ragged survivors and their few oxen, horses, and bicycles. And well-tended gardens and streets of flowering trees had replaced the monochrome of ash and debris. Though still a manufacturing city with a major seaport, the primary source of its prosperity, Hiroshima had become famous for its cut-flower industry and for its peace culture.

By 1981 the park contained close to a hundred memorials, a devastatingly effective A-bomb Memorial Museum, and an Atomic Culture Research Center. The hundreds of newly planted trees I remembered from my 1954 visit had grown into large, shady groves. The hundreds of white doves had become thousands, and the park had added scores of memorials.

Despite the Hibakusha's commitment to fostering world peace, for many, understandably, the wounds still festered. However, only at our hotel and in the Peace Park itself did Jane and I sense the slowly fading but palpable distaste for Americans that survives to this day.

I thought of the old couple at the Atomic Mound, shook my head, and ordered a refill for my hot chocolate. I needed the deliciousness of this self-medication. I thought I understood the relationship between my flu, jetlag, depression, and loneliness, but the perception failed to lighten my mood. All I could feel was the dark side of our human predicament. What life-stunting catastrophes might our children and grandchildren face because we failed to live up to our possibilities? What must we do? What must I do? And where to find the strength? Like a monster eating its own tail, the questions circled around and around in my aching body and numbed mind.

"Excuse me, sir."

Startled, I looked up to the left. The speaker wore black horn-rimmed glasses, a long-out-of-fashion tan suit, a white shirt, and a brown tie. His coal-black hair was slicked straight back with pomade.

I recognized the interpreter from the Atomic Memorial

Mound and rose to my feet. "Yes?" I asked. At first glance he appeared to be about my age, perhaps in his late fifties or early sixties, but bland and diffident almost to the point of invisibility—that is until he spoke.

"Good afternoon," he said, bowing slightly and smiling. "Please excuse me for break your peace."

Breaking what peace? I thought, but said, "That's quite all right, sir. May I help you?"

He smiled again and nodded, as if admitting the possibility. "But perhaps I may be of service to you." His voice was light but rich, resonant, as if somehow amplified.

"Thank you for your assistance at the Atomic Mound." I pointed to the empty chair. "Please. Join me." Though I wondered if the man might not be a local guide looking for work, I didn't care. I needed company.

"Thank you, sir." Bowing again, he sat, motioned to a waitress, and ordered coffee. "I am pleased to be of service," he said, then added, "I believe we share train from Osaka."

Yes, I thought, nodding, as I recognized the man from across the aisle. Amused and intrigued, I said, "So this is our third meeting?"

"What do you say in America? 'Third time is charm'?"

"Yes, close enough." I stuck out my hand by way of introducing myself. When the man declined to respond, I quickly withdrew it, remembering the Japanese distaste for shaking hands. "My name is Leonard Bird."

"I am Mr. Tanaka." He smiled briefly, pushed his coffee cup to the side, placed his knotty hands flat on the table, leaned forward, and stared directly into my eyes. I blinked a couple of times and returned the contact. "May I ask what brings you Hiroshima? Mr. Bird."

"Despair," I blurted, then shook my head to deny what I had just said and its pathetic, melodramatic tone. "I'm not quite sure. I've been here before, twice. I come in need, and in, ah, somewhat tremulous hope."

"*Ah so. Deseka*. I understand. Hope for what, Mr. Bird?"

At first the man seemed a bit too intent on peeling away my motives, like a CIA agent I once encountered in Belize City. I shook my head to dismiss the suspicion. Tanaka was far older than I'd first thought, probably well into his seventies. His pomaded hair was dyed, his face was a mask of fine lines, and his hands were gnarled by arthritis.

"Please excuse, Mr. Bird. Hope for what?"

Perhaps it was his age, perhaps his apparent interest, but I found myself trusting him. "I'm not quite sure," I replied, then poured out my ambivalence. "It has already been a very long day. I'm confused, unsettled. Many aspects of your park cut to the quick—horror, loss, despair, and, despite the despair, a deep commitment to peace. These things I see and feel, perhaps because I brought them with me."

"Yes. But it *is* the hope, Mr. Bird. Without hope we…"

"I don't feel it, and since I can't feel it, hope seems to be little more than an abstraction, like God or immortality."

Tanaka frowned and jerked back his head, as if my interruption had been a slap, but I continued on, far more upset than I had realized. "When it comes to the possibility for world peace, my logic dismisses hope as little more than the sterile fruit of naïveté."

"Ah, yes, Mr. Bird. There is real truth in what you say. But that is only one piece of truth. I think maybe you look for hope in wrong places."

"Perhaps." I shrugged, then asked a question that probably struck Tanaka as being more flippant than I intended. "Tell me, sir. Is hope something you carry in *your* toolbox?"

Seeming to ignore my question, Tanaka glanced around the room, then shut his eyes, frowned, and nodded. "Perhaps I should tell you something of myself."

"Please do."

"Yes." He blinked once and focused on his gnarled hands, which he'd locked together in front of him. "Most important are wife and daughter. I could never find their bodies."

"Excuse me!?"

"Maybe their ashes sleep in Atomic Mound."

"My God!" I interrupted. "I'm so..."

Tanaka frowned, shook his head, and continued. "Many in old neighborhood were too burned to recognize. Those first few days we cremate thousands nameless." Tanaka raised his gaze to meet mine, his eyes empty. "On Hiroshima Day, ten years after war, all nameless ashes move to Atomic Memorial Mound. That is why I visit, to feel close to wife and daughter. Once each month I come here from Osaka."

During Tanaka's toneless summary a chill crawled from my wet socks to the base of my neck. Tears came to my eyes. I wanted to take this old man in my arms and rock him against my chest, yet knew that his stiff, contained dignity would never allow such a familiar gesture. "I am deeply sorry," I mumbled, and reached out to cover his glacially cold hands with my newly warmed ones.

Instantly Tanaka pulled his hands away and placed them on his lap. "Thank you," he said, again gripping my soul with his eyes. "You ask, do I have hope as one of tools?"

"Well," I stammered, "Yes. I'm sorry. But how could you?"

Tanaka shook his head. "For myself? No. Since war I live alone. When I allow my spirit drift, it always return August 6, 1945, and next days and weeks and months. For long time I think to kill myself."

When I tried to interject more condolences, Tanaka again held up his hand. "But hope for world? Yes! For others? For the future? Yes! Many, many years I teach history. Because I believe education, because I believe people can learn more. Yes, I have a little hope."

He cocked his head slightly, as if trying to assess me from a different angle, and turned the question around. "Tell me, please, Mr. Bird, why can you not feel hope in our Peace Park?"

I took a sip from my mug, set it back on the table between my two hands and stared at it a moment before again raising my eyes. "I don't know. I just returned. From my last visit, twelve years ago, I glimpsed it, I guess."

Tanaka nodded emphatically. "This good place to find your hope."

"Yes, I guess I understand that, but..." I sounded like a fool but plunged on, talking as much to myself as to Tanaka. "Certainly, yes, I see hope, but only here and there. Hope is not missing, I guess, but it seems so tenuous, hard to grasp."

"Maybe that is nature of hope, yes?" Tanaka smiled. "At least you see. Yes, I think I might be of service."

Not quite sure how to respond, I clarified his earlier question. "You ask me why I came back? An almost desperate yearning for hope. That and the need to find a new sense of direction. I seem, somehow, to have lost my way.",

"Ah, yes. I suspect many stories in your 'somehow.'"

"Yes. Too many."

Tanaka nodded, glanced at his watch, then again seemed to change the subject. "You will still be Hiroshima tomorrow evening?"

"Yes, I don't have to leave until Sunday afternoon."

"Good. Then you can see our famous Hiroshima Flower Festival." Abruptly, Tanaka rose from his chair. "You will please meet me here five o'clock tomorrow evening. We will talk more about hope and where you might find it."

Somewhat disoriented by the abruptness of his declaration, I rose to my feet. "I will be here, Tanaka-san."

"Good, Mr. Bird. Good." Tanaka bowed formally and walked away.

Almost as soon as he disappeared from sight, I realized that something in my head had changed. Though I still felt alone, achy, and exhausted, my depression had lightened. I shook my head. I had just had a very direct conversation with a man who had lost everything, and I felt better? But no, not everything. The man seemed not to have lost his soul, and his words and presence had somehow nurtured me. I wanted to know more about him—his history, what he thought, felt, about the A-bombing, about the park, about life.

Later that evening, after a long bath and an unsettling nap, I sat at my small desk, gazed out at Central Station, and tried to recollect what I could remember of my first visit here so many years and lifetimes earlier. I remember with what innocent reluctance I undertook that distant train ride, and the degree to which the effects of that journey had hibernated until my descent into the trenches of Yucca Flat.

In 1954 Japan was still little more than a mountainous archipelago of poverty. With the exception of Kyoto, Nagano, and Kamakura, every major city had been heavily bombed, many repeatedly. In many cities, such as Tokyo, Osaka, Kobe, and Hiroshima, across hundreds of square blocks, tens of thousands of families struggled to live as cleanly and privately as possible in tiny, cobbled-together packing cases that were often covered by a sheet of corrugated tin. The geometrically aligned shanties showed poverty but not the squalor of most shantytowns. Everything looked neat, clean, and attended to.

In the countryside evidence of the war was less obvious. Since Japan's surrender had saved both her and her conquerors from the horrors of an extended land war, much of rural Japan seemed to have changed little from its prewar state. As is still the case, farm hamlets and market villages nestled in tight clusters around important river and rail crossings and between the extensive emerald terraces that climb the hills from upland valleys.

In its failed efforts to create and maintain an empire, Japan's militaristic government had sacrificed two generations of Japanese males. As is usually the case in wars initiated and fought by the politically powerful, most of those killed in the service of military and political hubris were peasants and factory workers. Both during the war and in the intervening nine years, women, children, and old men performed most of the work, heavy, menial, and otherwise, and much of the less-essential work went undone. Shops, while usually scrubbed clean, were often shabby and poorly stocked. Many farms were worn and unkempt. Though townspeople and farm folk had little money, they were better off by far than millions of city dwellers. Most of the former had enough to eat and adequate shelter. Though few owned cars or the money to fuel them, many families owned a bicycle. Clothing was drab—tan, brown, black, gray, olive—and worn, though usually clean and neatly mended. Of the men who had returned from the voracious maw of war, many still wore parts of their last uniform, again, faded and patched but clean.

The Korean War was just ending and America was preparing to abandon her numerous military bases around Japan, taking with her the dubious gift that the bases bestowed upon the local economies. Close to every military base, neighborhoods and small towns vied desperately for the dollars that American youth spent freely on liquor and women, both of which were cheap and plentiful. Widows, daughters, and sisters rented their bodies for a carton of American cigarettes to sell on the black market or for a few dollars' worth of military script.

Destitute Japanese veterans sold whatever service they could conceive, from washing American laundry to resoling combat boots. Regardless of what they must have been feeling as they literally begged for a pair of boots to shine or a few fatigues to wash, starch, and press, the Japanese veterans of whatever age always bowed repeatedly and smiled incessantly. They treated us as masters, and we enjoyed the role. After all, we felt, many of our fathers, uncles, and older brothers had fought and vanquished the "dirty Japs."

In 1954 I served in the Twelfth Marines, an artillery regiment permanently encamped just above tree line on the northern flank of Mt. Fuji. For better than a year, through typhoons and blizzards, I lived in a thirteen-man, wood-frame, canvas tent that sported a plywood floor and a kerosene-fed, potbellied stove. My closest friends were Begay and Washington. Partly because of his age but mostly because of his quiet yet insistent strength, Begay, a self-exiled Navajo, was our leader.

Eighteen-year-old high school dropouts who had been in trouble with the police, Washington and I had not joined the Marines in quest of world peace; neither of us had ever given the subject a serious moment's thought. Our motives were other. I had joined because I had been expelled from the eleventh grade less than halfway through the year; because I hated and needed to get away from my stepfather, with whom I was having fistfights; because I was lost and didn't know what to do; because I had seen too many "glory war" flicks;

and because the Marine Corps was the only branch of the service that would accept a high school dropout or juvenile delinquent, let alone someone who was both.

Washington, a black young man from rural Alabama, was far less confused about his motives for signing up. At mid-century the armed forces was one of the few sectors of American society in which minorities could rise according to their merits. Short but broad-shouldered, Washington had been a defiantly assertive high school fullback who almost suffocated in the poisoned air of Alabama. He enlisted in the Marines after sassing the wrong white man and serving time on a chain gang. Like me, to get into the Corps he first had to obtain a waiver from the Commandant of Marines.

As different as Washington and I were, a rural black Southerner and a white beach boy, we had more in common with each other than we did with Begay, whose quiet strength determined not only that we tag along with him to Hiroshima but also that we ultimately become far more than we might otherwise have become. Begay was a twenty-two-year-old, six-foot beanpole who had put in almost two years at an Arizona college. In Japan he spent most of his free time reading, working on a variety of college correspondence courses, and encouraging Washington and me to study for the high school GED test. Though the GED struck me at the time as an insurmountable mountain, Begay prevailed. Both Washington and I eventually passed it and later even enrolled in a couple of college correspondence courses.

What Begay had in common with Washington and me, in

addition to our slowly increasing interest in books and ideas, was his primary motive for becoming a Marine. Like many, if not most, Marine enlistees, Begay was running away. Late one night shortly before the end of his sophomore year in college, drunk and driving home from a rodeo, Begay had rolled his pickup and killed his cousin. A few weeks later he was a Marine "boot" in San Diego. Perhaps because of the accident that ended his cousin's life and launched his self-imposed exile from his extended family, Begay spent a lot of time thinking. Unlike Washington and me, he was interested in Japanese culture and sometimes dragged us along to Buddhist temples or Shinto shrines. And we tried, sometimes successfully, to drag him along on our testosterone-driven soirees to Yamanaka, Fuji-Yoshida, and Tokyo.

When Begay first proposed that we devote a precious three-day pass to Hiroshima, we were sitting atop a rock wall next to a teahouse, two thirds of the way up the summit of Mt. Fuji. Despite the arduousness of climbing the winding path and uneven stone steps, we felt strong, content, on top of the world. Far below us central Honshu spread out to the north and east as a concave plain that rolled down to the sea. At the foot of the mountain, just below tree line, Lake Yamanaka glistened in the midday July light.

Begay never went anywhere without a book, even up a mountain. While Washington and I were gazing out at the lake and swapping tales about two sisters who worked a dance hall in Fuji-Yoshida, Begay sat bent over his latest read, John Hersey's *Hiroshima*. Suddenly he placed the book reverently on the rock, extracted a Lucky Strike from its pack and tapped it slowly on the back of his hand. "You know what I think?"

"Oh, shit!" Washington mumbled. "For sure, trouble comin'."

What now? I thought. "Yes?"

"We're not going to Tokyo on our pass next week."

"What the hell makes you say that?" I asked, more amused than worried.

"We're going to Hiroshima. We need to do that. It's important."

"You want to go to Hiroshima?" I asked. "Didn't you see enough destruction in Korea? Haven't you seen enough in Japan?"

"Hiroshima is different," Begay said, lighting the Lucky and taking in the first deep draw.

Washington shook his head. "You're crazy, man. Why go there?"

"You'll see," Begay promised, staring out to the east toward Mishima and the ocean. "We are going there. Next weekend."

"No, Begay. You may be going to Hiroshima. Washington and I are going to Tokyo. You know? Like we planned?"

Begay just smiled, shook his head, and patted his book. "No! You need to read this book and we need to go there."

Both Washington and I tried to decline, and for what we thought to be adequate reasons. Throughout Japan, the ongoing presence of American servicemen was a running sore, a constant reminder of defeat, shame, and great loss. We knew how many, if not most, Japanese felt about our presence because we encountered the evidence in a variety of ways every time we left the base. Moreover, rumor had it that the survivors did not welcome Westerners, particularly Americans, and most particularly American servicemen.

Of course, our reluctance to go to Hiroshima involved more than the unpopularity of our presence; to that we had long become desensitized. But why pursue the morbid, we wondered? From Camp McNair we could instead bus half an hour west to Fuji-Yoshida, catch a four-hour train ride to Tokyo, and devote the weekend to some serious carousing. When it came to something Begay really wanted us to do, however, he usually won.

The humidity of late August intensified as, a few days later, we descended from the high northern flank of Mt. Fuji to the bustling railway town of Mishima, just above sea level. I remember the bus, crowded with shoppers, vegetables, and chickens; the tight switchbacks of the road that wound slowly down the mountain; the rich, seemingly impenetrable jungle of the lower slopes; and the impoverished hamlets and isolated shacks of those who lived in the deep gorges, too poor or landless to raise anything but a few vegetables and chickens. When the concave slope became gentler, we passed through emerald and jade terraces of ripening rice, and relatively more prosperous villages. I remember the women bending to harvest rice, and the occasional, nauseating pungency from the "night soil" or "honey buckets"—human waste used as fertilizer.

The route between Mishima and Hiroshima was essentially the same in 1954 as it is today, heading south along the Pacific coast, sandwiched between steep coastal mountains, and passing villages and terraces that descend to the sea. I remember the slowness of the train and the uncomfortable wooden seats, the shabbily dressed passengers, and the old, black-suited conductor with three gold front teeth. I remember the few prewar automobiles on mostly dirt roads, and the gray, rebuilding cities. Beyond that the journey itself is largely a blur. I spent most of the ride down and back lost in the noir pages of a Mickey Spillane novel.

Of Hiroshima, however, my memories, though few, are sharp—the cavernous train station, just beginning to rebuild nine years after the end of the war; the naked and twisted girders of the A-bomb Dome; and the newly opened and still mostly empty Park for World Peace. I remember the smallness of the park's newly planted trees, the hundreds of fluttering white doves, and the cenotaph, at that time the park's lone memorial. Probably because of its decades-long impact on my nightmares, one of the sharpest images from that distant visit is visual: a man's negative shadow etched on the side of a ruined concrete building. Except for the light silhouette behind where the man was sitting at the instant of his nuclear vaporization, the wall was dark, charred. A few years later when I first encountered a reproduction of Rodin's *The Thinker,* I flashed back to that negative shadow and the baffled emptiness I had felt when witnessing it. The shapes were the same.

I remember our two-kilometer walk west along the trolley line to the park's southern entrance. Everywhere we looked the Hibakusha were rebuilding, without power tools or large machines. I remember shabbily clad masons, many of them women, working from bamboo scaffolding, and wide, clean streets. Other than old bicycles and motor scooters, there were few vehicles. Building materials were carried by lines of workers or hauled on carts pulled by water buffalo or small horses. Though large parts of the old city were still without running water and sewers, the Hibakusha had in fact accomplished much. Fanning out from Central Station were several blocks of newly constructed two- and three-story buildings, often separated by wide vacant lots. On scores of other blocks new buildings were just beginning to rise from the ashes.

Another long-resonating image is visceral rather than visual and is itself a montage of observations and feelings: our inability to find a hotel, a woman pointing at us and hissing her anger, children turning away, and block upon block of four-foot-tall shanties. From across the river the serene park seemed to parody the surrounding poverty. The further west we ventured, the more open land we encountered, vacant lots and block after block of low hovels. Few people looked our way until we had passed, and none spoke. Though we wore Levis and short-sleeved shirts, we were not disguised. Our scalps were shaved, naked above the tan line that ran around our heads just an inch above the ear. Our spit-shined shoes shed light. We were Marines and walked erect and looked people in the eye. Even the mostly barefoot and obviously malnourished children hunkering down along the street fell silent as we three passed.

To my eighteen-year-old consciousness, the park seemed little more than a green Band-Aid taped over a world of ash. Blind to all but the human and material devastation, I wondered why the city hadn't put the money into housing rather than this large field of grass dotted with a few hundred trees and a couple of not-quite-finished buildings. I just didn't get it. Sad to say, from that first visit to the Peace Park I took away only two sharp reactions, both of which proved indelible: great awe at what one small atomic bomb can wreak, and a spine-chilling sense of what it means to be silently but obviously hated, not for what you yourself have done but rather for your nationality and what that nationality can so darkly symbolize. When we left Hiroshima I was depressed, angry at Begay, and certain I would never return.

Begay, Washington, and I served together until late 1957. We returned to the States, served in both the Fifth and Eleventh Marines at Camp Pendleton, and crouched next to each other in the trenches of Yucca Flat. As too often happens with good service buddies, however, once we were separated our friendship evaporated. I long ago lost track of Washington, as well as with Begay who, to my surprise, had decided to become "a lifer," to make the Marines a career. Twenty or so years ago, I heard that Begay was killed during his second tour in Vietnam.

I spent much of the evening groping back through a decades-thick mist and feeling profound gratitude for Begay's friendship. Had he not dragged me along on his pilgrimage to this place, my life would have been different and somehow lesser. And had it not been for Begay, I doubt that I would have left the Marines and gone to college. He encouraged us to read and study, and convinced us that we could become more than we had ever imagined and, at least in my case, far more than parents, teachers, or probation officers had expected. Except as it applied to his own life, Begay believed that, within our physical limitations, we can be anything in life that we want to be. Begay was wrong about that, of course. It was as if he had read too many Horatio Alger fantasies about the American dream. But for me, at least, Begay's quiet cajoling and philosophizing set a strong sense of direction.

✧ ✧ ✧

After a dream-plagued night I awoke clearheaded. The sky seemed a shade or two less gray. For the first time I could see all but the tops of the green hills that rise beyond the city. I felt stronger and looked forward to revisiting memorials I had yesterday passed by, and to meeting Tanaka later in the day.

Rather than riding all the way to the Aioi Bridge as I had the day before, I stepped from the trolley a few blocks short, crossed the Motoyasu River on East Peace Bridge, and entered the park, as it was designed to be entered, from Grand Peace Boulevard. The fifteen-meter-wide boulevard crosses the city from east to west. Unlike the northern end of the park, with its groves of trees and stands of bushes, the southern plaza is open, majestic, designed to pull the passerby into the park.

In the southern greenbelt of the park stand two memorials that have always seemed to me interconnected. The first opens the mind, the second the heart. At the southeastern entrance stands the Peace Tower, a concave, seamless pentagram molded like a single-peaked tent. The Peace Tower represents the five continents, devoid of national boundaries, finally melded. The premise? Only by moving closer to universal brother- and sisterhood can the world hope to transcend war and its various causes, such as prejudice, poverty, injustice, and fanaticism, and their tightly interwoven, mutually strangling effects. My problem lies not so much with the premise as with its desperate, precarious optimism.

Despite the fall of the Berlin Wall a few years earlier and the presumed end of history, more than a hundred armed conflicts, most of which are internecine wars among cousins, plague our shrinking and interdependent planet. In this new era of the terrorism wars, religious and political fanaticism cripples the possibility of diplomatic-economic-political solutions. Even in democracies, mere tolerance, let alone respect, remains beyond our grasp. Regardless, the Peace Tower symbolizes the right way: only through becoming less nationalistic and less culture-bound can we hope to survive.

More image than idea, the second memorial, *Mother and Children in the Firestorm,* speaks directly to the heart and requires no epigraph. Upon a large granite base, a cast bronze, twice-life-size mother struggles through the firestorm. Bent almost parallel to the ground by her burden, one arm slung low and behind to support the wounded son she carries on her back, the mother uses her free arm to shepherd along a second, younger child. Whenever I think of the One World premise latent in the very idea of the park, my heart leaps to this woman and her burden, a graphic symbol of the planet's countless refugees fleeing for their lives.

Immediately north of the heavily burdened but determined bronze mother stands the majestic Fountain of Prayer,
the centerpiece of the main entrance to the park. Through a
powerful composition of 567 jets, the fountain shoots eleven
tons of pastel-tinted water per minute. The resulting rainbow
sends to the heavens a prayer of lamentation and, in a light
breeze, sprays a fine mist over the statue of the struggling
mother and her two terrified children. The Hibakusha dedicated the fountain and its bounty to all those lost souls who
died athirst, "who died still pleading, *Mezu! Meee . . . zu.*"

With those words and the resonating image of fatally blistered mouths, I turned reluctantly toward the A-bomb Memorial Museum, a chamber of horrors and perhaps the site in the
park where but one hope shines: may memory suffice.

The spine of the park is a straight line of sight that con-
nects the statue of the mother and children at the southern end
with the Atomic Dome five hundred meters distant at the
northern end. Along that north–south line stand the Peace
Memorial Cenotaph, the Flame of Peace, and a long, narrow
pool that reflects the flame, the cenotaph, and the A-bomb
dome. The A-bomb Memorial Museum, which stretches west
to east, breaks that line, as if to emphasize the horrific alter-
native to world peace. Despite the raw symmetry of orchestrated mourning throughout the park, it is finally within the
walls of the museum that pilgrims grasp the reality of nuclear
holocaust. In this museum no hope shines, only horror.

The elevated, white, single-story building straddles the

main concourse that leads into the center of the park. Because it rests on huge concrete pillars, the museum seems to assault all who walk beneath and enter its shadow. Construction of the building began in the spring of 1951, the year before the embryonic park opened to the outside world. Because of the extreme poverty of the Hibakusha, however, the museum was unable to open until Hiroshima Day 1955, a year after my first visit.

In 1947 Shinzo Hamai, the newly elected mayor of Hiroshima, and Shogo Nagaoka, a part-time civil servant, encouraged the collection of thousands of pieces of human flotsam. Mayor Hamai believed that the collection would become an important witness to the holocaust, both a reminder and a warning. The exhibit halls bear mute testimony to the worthiness of Mayor Hamai's vision.[28]

Because images from my 1981 visit to the museum still wound my sleep, in 1993 I had to force myself up the long flight of stairs to again confront the dioramas, the hundreds of grainy black-and-white photographs, and the thousands of artifacts. Here exists little color, no serenity, and, again, no peace but for the dead. In these halls the anxious pilgrim confronts not memorials, epigraphs, prayers, and poems. Rather, here reside the physical images of the holocaust: display after display after display of scorched shoes and sandals, blackened pocket watches stopped at 8:16, and partly melted wedding rings; the twisted and charred frames of eyeglasses and fragments of military uniforms and equipment; the remnants of briefcases, walking canes, and appliances from homes, stores, and factories; and the charred, torn uniforms and blistered school satchels of the thousands of children and teachers who died on the firebreaks.

Even more than the assemblage of atomic detritus, it is the photographs and dioramas that grip, appall, and terrify. The hundreds of often underexposed photographs, most taken within hours or a few days of the blast, create a frontal confrontation with our nuclear legacy so ghastly that the denying mind retreats into delusion.

Of the dioramas I remembered from my 1981 journey, two were etched into my mind and became recurring motifs in my nightmares. The first presents the inferno from on high. In the middle of the main, circular gallery stands a circular black model of central Hiroshima shortly after the blast. Across the narrow hall stand dioramas that are more personal, and far more horrifying. Like speechless and impotent gods, pilgrims stand above the model, look down on Little Boy's hypocenter, down on the seven rivers that flow from the crescent of hills into Ujina Harbor, and down upon the four-thousand-meter-diameter zone of total destruction. Regardless of where one stands around that model, one cannot look up without confronting the surrounding dioramas, where each desperate figure, burning through time, stares back.

In the most searing diorama, terror-stricken families flee the fires. Half-naked, burned, and bloody, life-size and lifelike, victims struggle toward the viewer, many with their arms out in front of them, palms up, as if beseeching relief. The central figure of the diorama is a mother. Sheets of skin and plasma hang from her naked chest. Her arms cradle a dead, charred infant. Her open mouth howls silently. Like countless other mothers before, since, and to come, that mother's fate was not just to die in the cataclysm but, worse, to witness the loss of all she loves. In the months that followed my 1981 visit, this anonymous mother became a central image in "The Survivor."

As I again gazed down on the ruined city and the small red light that represents the hypocenter, memory jerked me back to the Nevada desert, where I was caught in the ever-shifting nightmare that was Shot Hood. I felt dizzy, shut my eyes, leaned on the railing, and remembered.... We crouched in the bottom of the trench as the thunder of nuclear wind swept over our heads. An instant later we stood near ground zero and tried not to breathe the dust that swirled around us. Then I was standing in a Quonset hut, shedding my contaminated clothing and shivering with dread as I waited for the next available shower and a bar of harsh soap. I was again back in the trench, crouched next to my buddies. Somewhere a deep voice growled, "Stand up and face ground zero! Stand up and face ground zero!"

Hyperventilating and sweating, I opened my eyes. A museum guard stared my way, his concern obvious. I stumbled from the room as quickly as possible and headed for open air. As soon as I reached the bottom of the stairs and the first empty bench, I sat down, put my head between my legs, and breathed deeply. The clouds had again lowered, and a fine mist fell. The mist on my bare neck was a cool caress.

In great need of relief from the depression that again

FIGURE 6. A-bombed Teacher and Student, International Park for World Peace, Hiroshima. Monoprint by Jane Leonard.

weighed me down, I approached the Peace Memorial Cenotaph, the park's oldest and central memorial. Like an ancient,
open-ended shelter, a simple bronze-and-concrete arch protects a stone sarcophagus against sun and rain, and against
our tendency to forget. The black granite sarcophagus con-
tains the names of more than 140,000 victims. Since some of
the Hibakusha have taken a long time to die, the list continues
to grow. Engraved on the front of the sarcophagus is a simple
prayer and the park's most profound pledge:

LET ALL THE SOULS HERE REST IN PEACE,
FOR WE SHALL NOT REPEAT THE EVIL.

I stood before the black sarcophagus and gazed through
the arch, beyond the reflecting pool and Atomic Flame to the
twisted steel skeleton of the Atomic Dome. At the southern
end of the park, the dark reality of the Atomic Museum con-
trasts with the more hopeful memorials. At the northern end
the Atomic Dome provides a dramatic backdrop for the cenotaph and its promise of peace.

I sat on a low wall and watched the few visitors, all Japanese, approach the cenotaph, read the plaque, and bow their
heads. I thought again of my first visit here so many years earlier and of my inability then to grasp the vision or appreciate
the sacrifice. "Not repeat the evil." The "we" includes not
only Japan, which started the war, and America, which finished it. The "we" includes all those who stand before this sarcophagus, bow their heads in mourning, and make the com-

FIGURE 7. Cenotaph, International Park for World Peace, Hiroshima. Monoprint by Jane Leonard.

mitment to somehow, however haltingly, work toward world peace and its prerequisites, tolerance and justice.

After gazing at the sarcophagus and mouthing the words, I raised my head, stared at the A-bomb Dome, then focused on the middle distance and the Flame of Peace. Nowhere in the park can one find a stronger example of the determination permeating Hiroshima's peace culture than in this flame, designed to burn until we defuse the last nuclear weapon, however distant that time may be. Tragically, the further we move from Hiroshima and August 6, 1945, the greater the hurdles become. Hatred, fanaticism, and national arrogance are on the ascendant and nuclear weapons continue to proliferate.

In the afternoon the clouds thinned and the intermittent showers ceased. Almost on cue, the park seemed to fill, as if the hundreds of shoppers in the Han Dori Mall and elsewhere were merely biding their time. In less than an hour the hundreds of doves again became thousands, as they ventured from beneath the shrubbery to strut across the grass or flutter in flocks from one part of the park to another. For an hour or so, like the doves, I floated from memorial to memorial until the various epigraphs forged a litany of entangled despair, hope, and wishful thinking.

I looked at my watch and took a deep breath. Hours were running short. I cut across the park to the memorial for Sankichi Toge, a founder of the A-bomb school of poetry. Toge's memorial is one of his simple poems, "Give Back the Human," etched on a large cube of black granite. The cube rests on an altar-like base under the protection of a cherry tree whose sodden blossoms mottled the wet ground pink.

> GIVE BACK MY FATHER, GIVE BACK MY MOTHER;
> GIVE GRANDPA BACK, GRANDMA BACK.
> GIVE ME MY SONS AND DAUGHTERS BACK.
> GIVE ME BACK MYSELF.
> GIVE BACK THE HUMAN RACE.
> AS LONG AS THIS LIFE LASTS, THIS LIFE,
> GIVE BACK PEACE THAT WILL NEVER END.

"Give me back myself?" When Little Boy exploded over central Hiroshima, the young poet was writing in his house in Midori-mochi, slightly beyond the zone of total destruction. As happened to thousands of others who thought they had survived the bomb, Toge developed radiation sickness. And like so many others who suffered from the wasting anemia,

Toge did not get better, though perhaps he did get back his "self." Although bedridden much of the time until his death at age thirty-six, Sankichi Toge continued to craft into poetry both his personal despair and his quiet hope for world peace.[29]

I stared at Toge's poem, at words simple to the point of enigma. What he wanted, what he died yearning for, is clear— life, family, peace. Though most of the data seem to indicate that hope is often no more than yearning born of desperation, our hearts, of course, tell us otherwise. Hope is everything. Not until my final departure from the park the next afternoon would I finally come to understand, and feel, that hope is a process, albeit not always a logical one. Hope is integral to the psyche. Like the English Romantic poet John Keats, who also wasted away at a young age, Toge seems to have been moved by a powerful realization: Truth, beauty, despair, hope, and mortality weave into a strong thread.

For another hour or so I sat on the bench before Sankichi Toge's "prayer" and observed other tourists and the few old women Hibakusha who still tend the park. While the Tower of a Thousand Cranes and its deeply piled origami look to the future and personify our hope for world peace, the sight of the lonely old women trigger a far different realization: they have little to dwell on but a life-shattering past already half a century gone, that and the long emptiness of their lives.

In 1981 Jane and I were sitting on this same bench, mesmerized by Toge's desperate, hopeless prayer. A bent old woman carrying a twig broom entered the circle to sweep away a few leaves and a tissue. She wore a faded pink, long-sleeved cotton blouse, baggy black pantaloons, a long white apron, and white cotton gloves. A wide-brimmed straw hat completely shaded her head. When she approached Toge's poem, the old woman read it slowly, almost as if she had never before seen the words. She turned her head and stared briefly at Jane and me before turning back to Toge's memorial. A moment later she continued on her rounds. Her deep-set, obsidian eyes seemed to reflect the quiet despair of her life. I have since often wondered, what was she thinking? What was her private response to the horror wrought by America's Little Boy? How did she relate to the Peace Park and its various sentiments and to the few Americans and Europeans who venture here? What are their motives, she must have wondered. What are they looking for? How dare they!

In "The Survivor" the old woman metamorphosed into Fumiko Matsumi, a former schoolteacher whose entire class of thirteen- and fourteen-year-old girls was incinerated at the firebreaks of Zaimoku-cho. Miss Matsumi's loneliness ended only with her death. In "The Survivor" she tastes the despair latent in Toge's prayer. With far more bitterness than acceptance, she moans,

> Nothing is given back.
> All is changed, forever changed.
> All that we love has burned away.

Later I met Tanaka as planned. In deference to his age, his status as a Hibakusha, and my respect for him personally, I arrived at the Sweden Restaurant ten minutes early, only to find him already seated. Other than a freshly starched white shirt, the old man was dressed as before. He rose from his chair, smiled, and refused to sit until I had taken my seat. After we greeted each other, he placed his hands flat on the table and again, in very un-Japanese fashion, stared into my eyes.

"Yesterday I said maybe I can be of service. I have thought about that a little."

I raised my eyebrows. "So have I."

"Good!" He nodded briefly then seemed to change the subject. "At the Atomic Mound? I think you wanted to say something to that old woman you upset. May I ask, is that not truth?"

"Well...yes, Tanaka-san, but..." He waited, smiling slightly. "All right. I first came here in 1954, as a young Marine. Almost exactly three years later I was an involuntary,

FIGURE 8. Sankichi Toge Monument and Hibakusha Sweeper, International Park for World Peace, Hiroshima. Monoprint by Jane Leonard.

nuclear guinea pig...." I gave him a brief description of what I had experienced at Yucca Flat and concluded: "A few hours after the blast, unprotected by anything but a World War II gas mask, I stood within two hundred meters of ground zero. I remember standing there with my buddies, trying to mask our fear with jokes, as clouds of irradiated dust swirled by." I stopped for a moment and nodded, pleased to be able to say what I felt. "To some degree, at least, it is kinship that brings me here. That and my fears for my grandchildren. I feel strongly connected to this city and particularly to your Park for World Peace."

Tanaka looked at me for a long time before nodding. "I am glad you have grandchildren. Your god has been good to you. I sorrow you had such meeting with A-bomb, and my heart sorrow more for America. But also, sir, you must know. *Nothing* you experience with your A-bomb, regardless of size, can compare what happen here and Nagasaki. You understand?"

"I know that," I mumbled defensively, embarrassed that the man felt it necessary to make the point. "No. It is not the same. Yucca Flat changed my life in some major ways and set me down on another track, but from that track has come some good. Like you, I am a teacher, and I know that what I experienced at Yucca Flat—and here in Hiroshima—has had a good effect on what and how I teach."

Tanaka nodded. "Perhaps it would have been better for world if all Americans had go to Yucca Flat."

I shuddered. "I don't know about that. But I do know that it would be good for everybody in the world to come here.

Yet... most of my countrymen spend a lot of time and money avoiding what they perceive to be morbid."

Tanaka shook his head. "My countrymen too. Maybe all of us, yes? We avoid important reality. Maybe it is your job help people see more clear." He squinted his already narrow eyes, as if appraising me, then smiled and continued. "If I may say so, Mr. Bird, your country maybe has too great power and too little wisdom. Now that America has won Cold War I hope your great power does not make you too proud and too blind."

"Me too, Tanaka-san. But... " I paused.

He raised his eyebrows. "Yes?"

"Wisdom sometimes leads to power. But how often has great power led to wisdom? Without a whole lot of pain for a whole lot of people?"

Tanaka again jerked a short nod and immediately changed the subject, as if the nod had said it all. "I will now tell you something about hope. Hope comes from belief that world can change, if only by few people at a time. In our peace culture we believe people can be taught to see new peace vision."

"But in time?" I asked.

"Your Jesus said we will never know the time until it comes. In the meantime we light our lamps. In Buddhism, too, light is necessary. It is important to shed a little light."

I shook my head. "I like to believe that, sir. What I try to do as a teacher is grounded in that belief. Change is possible! However... "

"Yes, Mr. Bird. No 'however.' Hope people can change is life raft. We must not let go. Also, I think maybe you have change."

I nodded, both sobered and amused to flash back over the past forty-five years to my delinquent teens in East San Diego, my suspension from school and the long tour in the Marines, and the meandering paths and detours I had since traveled. More, I thought about the mistakes I had made and the irreparable harm I had done along the way.

Tanaka seemed to be reading my mind. "Yesterday I told you about my family. I am sorry if I bore you, but may I tell you a little more about self?"

I raised my hands in relief and supplication. "Please!"

"I have not always been teacher. You should know, I was captain in Imperial Army. I am one of those who help my country destroy itself. In process we destroy many, many others."

"That is a very direct assessment," I said, embarrassed by Tanaka's candor and obvious sadness.

"It is also truth. In 1938 I return from three years in California, where I study American history. I had, excuse me for say so, felt too much rudeness from your countrymen." Tanaka's tone was flat, unemotional, matter-of-fact. "Because I, too, need to prove to world that we Japanese are no inferior to great white race, I join Imperial Army. After officer school I spend four years in China and do things to blacken my heart. In 1944 I was transfer Hiroshima, my family home."

At a loss for words, I nodded. Our eyes remained locked, and neither of us said anything for what seemed like a long minute.

"This, too, you should know. Certainly I wish you had not drop your A-bombs on us, but I no longer feel anger or bitterness. I think President Truman want to save American lives."

"Excuse me, sir?" I could not quite grasp the switch in topic, or Tanaka's apparent detachment from what he had just said. President Truman's decision had destroyed his life. "Of course he wanted to save American lives," I said. "Still... pardon me for saying so, Tanaka-san, but many historians and ethicists look at the question quite differently. Some Americans are horrified by our use of the bomb and the precedent we thus established. Even more Americans are appalled by what we did to Nagasaki just three days later. Some critics feel that we should have given your government more time to respond to the flattening of Hiroshima. However, given the horrific realities of battles to win Iwo Jima and Okinawa and the then perceived options... "

"Whether second bomb, or even first, was necessary I can not judge. But you must know, Mr. Bird, even after Nagasaki, general staff resist surrender. Had not emperor intervene and order surrender, war would have continue and you would have invade. Japan is very much mountain. War would have lasted a long time. I think maybe you learn that in Vietnam, yes?"

"Before invading Japan we would have dropped a third bomb. If necessary we would have built and dropped a fourth and fifth. That's how desperate we were to avoid invading Kyushu that November."

Tanaka smiled. "You are good student, Mr. Bird. Yes, that is point. No leader in world would not have use.... Excuse me. Not just Truman. Any leader of any country would do same."

"Then how can you remain so stoic...?"

"Please, listen. In circumstance, Truman had no choice. He had to use bomb. To believe otherwise is fool's job. To spare your country more dead and wounded, President Truman would have drop another A-bomb. I agree. He had two goals: gain from Japan total surrender, and save American lives. Your A-bombs accomplish two goals, yes?"

It upset me that Tanaka seemed so coldly logical in his analysis of Truman's decisions, though I tended to agree with his arguments. "With all due respect," I started.

Tanaka held up his hand. "It is not our purpose to settle debate. We do not have tools—or wisdom. That is not our work, is it?"

"No." I was relieved to move away from what had become an academic subject. "The future will be determined by what we humans do now, here and now, in the present."

Tanaka smiled, as if he had completed a simple lesson with a difficult student. "Yes, Mr. Bird. Past shed confusing light on present. Again, necessary to shed a little light, *ne!*" Maybe that is why we become teachers.

I chuckled. "It sounds good, though maybe a little self-serving."

Tanaka shrugged. "I have for you another truth. I think maybe it is also promise."

"Please."

As he had done the afternoon before, Tanaka rose abruptly from his chair and grabbed his raincoat. I pushed back from the table and almost leaped up.

"Excuse me," I said, trying to suppress the panic in my voice. "I thought…"

"Please excuse. I tire easy, Mr. Bird. I must rest now."

"I'm sorry, sir. I didn't mean to keep you."

Tanaka bowed his head slightly in acknowledgment, then held his hand up to his chest, raised his index finger straight up, wagged it twice, and said, "Tomorrow I think you will open your eyes to different truth, and find your hope. I think maybe you just need open eyes a little wider. See all the flowers." And with that instruction, he smiled again, bowed, and turned away.

For a moment or so after Tanaka disappeared, I stared in the direction of his retreating back. Though he walked ramrod straight, like the Army officer he had once been, Tanaka walked slowly, stiffly. I counted backward and forward from 1938, the year Tanaka claimed to have returned from his disillusioning years in California, and figured that he must be close to eighty. I beckoned the waitress to bring me a cup of hot chocolate. I wasn't sure what Tanaka had given me, but it certainly wasn't what I had expected.

In the years since that conversation, I have come more fully to understand that how one judges President Truman's decision to drop Little Boy and Fat Man depends more on one's viewpoint than on any major disagreement about the facts. Did America's decision to unleash the dragons of nuclear warfare alter the shape and tenor of the world, perhaps forever? Yes. Did the decision save hundreds of thousands of American lives and innumerable Japanese lives as well? Probably. Did it immediately put an end to further carnage in Asia and Oceania and bring our boys home? Obviously.

Presidents Roosevelt and Truman seldom mentioned winning the war without yoking that win to the blood of America's youth and the need to staunch the flow. The popular journals divided their content between the war news (always censored), and features designed to buoy homeland morale. Increasing numbers of mothers and wives hung single or double or sometimes even three-star flags in their front windows, a blue star per son or daughter or husband at war, and a gold star for one killed in action.

I remember walking home from school one day sometime late in the war. Tommy Allen was with me. We had spent half an hour in detention because of something to do with a game of marbles. Tommy's brother was in the Navy, somewhere in the Pacific. As we hopped up onto Tommy's front porch, we saw his mother's hand reach in front of the lace curtains. She removed the flag with the blue star. A moment later her hand, shaking, reappeared to hang a gold star.

Given the incredible costs of finally vanquishing Germany just two months earlier, and the increased ferocity of the Pacific War as we fought our way closer to Japan's home islands, America—leaders, fighting men, and civilians alike—dreaded the planned land invasion of Japan. Despite the end of the war in Europe, increasing numbers of gold stars were appearing in windows. The surviving veterans of Europe were preparing to transfer to the Pacific War. Everyone knew that tens of thousands of young men who had graduated from high school in

1943 and 1944 had already disappeared into the grinding maw of replacement battalions on the German front.

Because of Japan's mountainous terrain and the discipline of its people, a land invasion of Japan would prove to be far worse. American strategists presumed that invasions of Kyushu in November and Honshu in April would result in close to a million American casualties. In Germany the Allies did not have to fight the populace; in Japan they would. Despite the enormity of the decision to use A-bombs, it would have been politically impossible for the leader of any country, free or otherwise, not to use a weapon seemingly guaranteed to end the war. That is, of course, the short-term view, blind to all but the most desperately pressing need. Unfortunately for the welfare of the species, in times of crisis it is the short-term view that prevails.

I left the Sweden Restaurant, re-crossed the river, and headed back through the park. Somehow I had forgotten to visit the Tamiki Hara Memorial, which stands in a small, almost hidden copse on the east side of the Atomic Dome. Twelve years earlier Hara's poem, etched on a white granite cube, had set the tone of "The Survivor."

> ENGRAVED IN STONE LONG AGO,
> LOST IN THE SHIFTING SAND,
> IN THE MIDST OF A CRUMBLING WORLD,
> THE VISION OF ONE FLOWER.

Already depressed by the premature death of his wife and the devastation of Hiroshima, Tamiki Hara committed suicide in 1951, shortly after learning that the Americans were seriously considering atomic warfare in Korea. That suffering on the scale he had witnessed might afflict another community was more than the young poet could bear.[30]

Despite the prevailing note of despair that weaves through his poems, Tamiki Hara's "vision of one flower" did miraculously bloom. The year after his death, on Hiroshima Day 1952, the International Park for World Peace opened its arms to a war-weary but still fratricidal world. The Hibakusha had not transcended their despair so much as integrated it and turned it to strength. Like Tanaka, I thought. Like Tanaka.

❧ ❧ ❧

On the final day of that last visit I opened my eyes to the brightness of a clear sky. For a moment I thought I was back home, awakening to an almost seamless array of sunny days. But then I heard the already raucous traffic from the street below, and knew. My home in southwestern Colorado is four miles from a paved road. There the most intrusive sounds are those of squawking magpies and yapping coyotes.

After a few minutes of stretching and a quick bath, I boarded the 7:30 trolley, stopped at the Han Dori Mall for a light breakfast, and entered the park with a growing sense of excitement. My mood of the previous day had lightened even more. I had slept deeply and was feeling much stronger and determined to open my eyes "a little wider," as Tanaka had not so subtly suggested.

Even before crossing the Motoyasu River, I could hear the deep toll of the Peace Bell, striking every half minute or so and resonating through the surrounding neighborhoods. I walked to the lily pond that surrounds the bell and sat on a bench beneath a large tree in fresh leaf. A silent, reverent line of pilgrims awaited their turn to bow to the Goddess of Peace and ring the bell. Above the trees the roofless and tortured girders of the Atomic Dome seemed to brood over the bright morning. Yet all around me the sights and sounds and smells of spring bore witness to rebirth. I turned my back on my deep-rooted pessimism and joined the line.

The twelve-hundred-kilogram bronze bell is engraved with a map of the world that shows continents and islands—but no national boundaries. The belfry, representing the universe, is an open concrete dome supported by four pillars. In many ways the map on the Peace Bell mirrors the seamless pentagram of the Peace Tower at the southern end of the park, and the vision of one world—of diverse, tolerant, and cooperative brother- and sisterhood. Tragically for all concerned, one-world themes absolutely enrage increasing multitudes of fanatics—racial, ethnic, and religious "true believers"—that is to say, the most dangerous people on the planet.

I bowed, approached, grabbed the massive, iron-ringed, pine hammer with both hands and slammed it full force. Though I had rung the bell twelve years earlier, I had forgotten its power. The deep *GOONNGGG* resonated as a shock wave through my body and reverberated through the park. "Please," I prayed to the power and wisdom of the universe,

FIGURE 9. Peace Bell, International Park for World Peace, Hiroshima. Monoprint by Jane Leonard.

wherever and whatever it might be. "Please, God, before it is too late, please, God, grant us a clearer vision and greater strength." Though my faith was and remains weak, the prayer and the hope welled up from my deepest core.

"*Dozo!*" said the person standing patiently behind me. I shook my head, bowed, and apologized for taking so much time. As I walked away I became even more aware of the beauty of this Sunday morning. As the thousands of fallen cherry blossoms dried, the morning breeze pushed and swirled them in low, floating eddies. Yesterday I had been all but oblivious to the life flowing through the park. Today had already brightened into a multicolored world of movement—blossoms, doves, and people choreographed against a backdrop of green. Already there were far more people in the park than I had seen in the previous two days, and far more families, often moving in small clusters that represented several generations. Many of the children and some adults wore garlands of origami cranes around their necks. Some of the children carried pennants or balloons shaped like carp, the traditional symbol of Children's Day.

The tempo, too, was changing. Everywhere I sensed festivity, celebration, joy. Most of the passersby were striding rapidly toward the southern end of the park. In the distance I heard the music of a marching band. Remembering Tanaka's allusion to the Flower Festival, I headed south toward the park's main entrance and found myself in a rapidly increasing throng.

The Hiroshima Flower Festival begins with an exuberant parade that marches along Grand Peace Boulevard. As far as I could see, east or west, thousands upon thousands of citizens lined both sides of the boulevard. As is the case with parades everywhere, children were allowed up front, people in the rear craned their necks, and fathers held toddlers on their shoulders.

At first I was confused by the juxtaposition of this loudly festive mood and the tragic motifs of the Peace Park. We stood on sacred ground. In my mind's eye I saw the cenotaph and its somber vow and heard the grieving despair of Toge's prayer. It seemed, at first, as if a rock band were playing in the holy sepulcher. I was tempted to flee to the quiet, reflective beauty of the park. A few minutes later, however, I laughed aloud at my arrogance. As a dim light brightened, I sensed the obvious. The Hiroshima Flower Festival is a constellation of synchronous events: it heralds Golden Week, Japan's longest holiday, and Children's Week, one of its most important. Like most spring festivals, this one celebrates rebirth in all its riotous glory—flowers, birds, children. And on this day the citizens of Hiroshima celebrate their communal metamorphoses, first through pain and despair but finally through a clear vision and great will. The festival resonates at a profound level, between bitterness over an apocalyptic past and commitment to a more enlightened future; between joy and melancholy. The dominant tone celebrates new life and our capacity for joy.

It seemed that almost everyone in Hiroshima who belonged to a community organization of any sort had donned their most festive garb and joined the parade. A multicolored banner preceded each group: Mitsubishi factory workers, women's literary clubs, Cub Scouts and Brownies, seam-stresses, schoolteachers, marching bands, acrobats, rock-and-roll groups, and a quartet of drummers pounding away on two giant drums mounted on a semitrailer. Many of the marchers wore sashes or armbands proclaiming the group's motto or purpose. People chatted or sang as they marched, obviously proud of their organizations and community. For two clamorous and smiling hours the procession marched proudly along Grand Peace Boulevard. The intertwined themes of hope and gratitude wove together the long parade of marching citizens, blaring bands, flower-bedecked floats, and tens of thousands of delighted onlookers.

When the parade ended, some of the crowd streamed into the park, first to purchase food from the scores of white tents that dotted its southern edges, and then to wander toward the Atomic Memorial Museum and its plaza. From one of the booths I purchased a bowl of sukiyaki and a liter of ice water, then sat at a long table where I was soon joined by a family of youngish parents and three girls. The parents smiled and bowed and the girls immediately launched into an intermittent and repetitive chorus of "Herro. How are you? I fine" that lasted until I finished my lunch and rose, chuckling, to leave the tent. A chorus of "good-byes" trailed after me.

A growing crowd flowed through the entrance toward the central courtyard, where workers had erected a large stage and sound system, literally in the shadow of the A-bomb Museum. The Flower Festival is an act of love, an offering of thanks to the sacrificed dead, who have been transformed into conduits of peace. But above all, the festival is a celebration of new life and new hope.

From time to time, mist from the fountain reached out as if to caress the crowd, and a warm breeze wafted the subtle scent of flowers. In a semicircle around the stage, hundreds of children sat or squatted on the concrete. Everyone else stood, just as they had stood through the long parade, many with toddlers perched on their shoulders or asleep in backpacks.

Again I was confused. The Hibakusha had located the bandstand literally in the shadow of the A-bomb Memorial Museum. And that, of course, is their point. Like few people on earth, the survivors and their descendants grasp the tension between extremes of human action and emotion. Beneath a museum of horror, a new spring danced. The variety show featured local talent: folk dancers, drummers, singers, rock bands, magicians, choirs, and more, many of whom had marched in the parade. As I watched and listened, I felt the pride of those surrounding me. It was palpable, communicable. They had not only built a new city. They had envisioned and built a new culture.

Finally aware that I had little more than an hour left to spend in this darkly yet beautifully sacred spot, I left the crowd, passed again between the pillars of the A-bomb Museum, and headed into the grassy areas of the park. Before leaving Hiroshima I wanted to pray at the cenotaph, wander the paths just once more, spend a few more minutes at the Children's Monument, and again ring the Peace Bell.

I joined the short line of pilgrims waiting to pray at the

cenotaph and almost immediately recognized the couple a few feet in front of me, the old man and woman I had encountered at the Atomic Memorial Mound two days earlier. Momentarily recaught in the loneliness and alienation I had brought with me to Hiroshima, I thought of just walking away. But when they turned and recognized me, the tiny, hunchbacked woman immediately smiled and nodded. My anxiety faded. When their turn came, the old couple bowed before the black sarcophagus and its 140,000 names. After a long minute the old man put his arm around his wife and led her away.

I thought again of having stood in this precise spot thirty-nine years earlier. As a young Marine very confused by my surroundings, I remember reading the prayer, which I did not quite understand, and staring out beyond the newly planted trees to the ruin of the Atomic Dome and to the thousands of low shanties that had surrounded the new park. Again I remembered being struck by the insanity of a project that put the need for a park ahead of the need for human shelter. Not until my first return decades later did I come to see that the two knit together: the Hibakusha's profound commitment to peace and their steel-jawed determination to see their dead as sufficient sacrifices to Kannon, the Goddess of Peace, fueled their journey back from death to new life.

When my turn came, I stood before the cenotaph and read again the words carved on the front of the sarcophagus.

LET ALL THE SOULS HERE REST IN PEACE,
FOR WE SHALL NOT REPEAT THE EVIL.

The prayer embodies the basic tensions one finds in the park, sorrow, commitment—and hope, that vulnerable but tenacious and most essential of emotions. It was, after all, not their horror, shock, and despair that drove the Hibakusha to rebuild as a World Federalist city. Nor was it despair that moved them to dedicate nonexistent resources to this beautiful burial ground. Rather, it was hope, hope that new children would come, that it was indeed possible to build a new life, and that the park might promulgate a new vision of what the world can and must become. Surely, they must have thought that if we can envision a better world then we can create it.

As I wandered through the park for the last time on this clear, breezy afternoon, I attended to sound and its various levels and tones—the music from the stage show on the southern side of the A-bomb Museum, the almost-incessant tolling of the Peace Bell to the north, and the softer sounds in between: the erratic breeze as it moved through the lightly rubbing branches and leaves, the fluttering doves circling in droves, and the murmuring conversation and laughter of the clusters of families who occupied the benches, played on the grass, or strolled from memorial to memorial.

In many ways more relaxed than the Japanese families I had encountered in the fifties, contemporary families handle children like Americans, that is to say in a variety of ways. On this particular day, some families stayed very close together, their one or two children tightly controlled. Other families allowed their children to run. Many romped in the grass, chasing each other, turning somersaults, or kicking soccer balls back and forth.

I kept one eye out for Tanaka and his brown suit. Though he had said nothing specific, I felt he would appear. Before heading over to the Children's Memorial and its piled strings of paper cranes, I decided to stop once more at the Atomic Memorial Mound, where Tanaka believed the ashes of his wife and daughter were entombed. For a long while I stood back among the trees, observed the mourners that circled the mound, and thought of the words carved at the base of another memorial: "They rest here, the foundation of a peaceful world." The underlying, essential, and problematic premise is that we can learn from Hiroshima and Nagasaki and can build a more enlightened world. That is the prayer, that is the commitment. And there is the hope.

I stopped to watch two small boys, perhaps a year or so apart but dressed identically in blue shorts and Winnie-the-Pooh T-shirts. As fast as they could scoop, the boys gathered handfuls of dry cherry blossoms, held their cupped hands before their mouths and blew them in each other's face. My sudden appearance slowed them for but a moment. When I laughed, caught back in my own childhood, one of the boys turned and blew his blossoms in my direction. Immediately, I scooped up a few and blew them back. I heard other laughing and turned to discover a couple sitting on a nearby bench. Red-faced, I stood straight up and tried to appear dignified, which caused the woman, who was covering her mouth with her hand, to laugh harder. The father called two names and the boys ran over and circled the bench a couple of times before settling down. The youngest clamored into his mother's lap.

"*Konnichiwa,*" I smiled. "Good afternoon."

"Good aftanoon," the father said, nudging his wife, who was still trying to suppress her laugh. "We tink-a maybe you like our boys."

"Yes. I used to be one." We laughed and I nodded my head toward the boys. "I have grandchildren their age."

"*Ah so.* That is happiness, *ne!*" The wife whispered something to her husband, who nodded. "My wife say, 'Tank-a you for praying wif boys,' and she say, 'tank-a you for coming Hiroshima.' I say too."

Something within me opened like a bud. "Thank you very, very much," I said, bowing deeply. "I am very glad I came." At that moment my fears and preoccupations surrendered to a heady rush of exhilaration, one of those rushes of appreciation that make our lives precious and make avoidable suffering tragic.

I walked to the Children's Peace Memorial with more real joy than I had felt since leaving home. Even so, I was unprepared for what proved to be my final encounter in Hiroshima. Just yesterday the Tower of a Thousand Cranes had been deserted. After three days of rain, the sodden origami cranes had bled most of their color. Today resembled more that sunny June day, twelve years earlier, when Jane and I had watched scores of uniformed students present their brightly colored offerings.

A few old people and half a dozen families stood in small clusters or sat along the low wall that frames Sadako's memorial. A boy wearing white shorts and shirt and carrying a string of rainbow-colored cranes approached the already deeply piled offerings. Several other children waited to place their own strings. They stood silently or talked in quiet tones to their parents and siblings.

As I watched the slow procession of offerings to Kannon and to the soul of twelve-year-old Sadako Sasaki, who had folded her cranes and died of radiation sickness so many years before, I thought of the prayer carved at the base of the memorial by another middle school student many years later: "This is our cry. This is our prayer. For building peace in this world." I thought of all the other students of Sadako's generation, some killed by the blast and fires, others living for ten or twenty years before finally succumbing to radiation poisoning. As this new generation of young people placed their wreaths of fresh hope, I inhaled the perfumed beauty of Children's Day and prayed for my grandchildren.

A girl in her early teens carrying a strand of flamingo-colored cranes detached from her parents and approached Sadako's memorial. Dressed in a blue and green plaid skirt and green blouse, the girl moved with assured grace. She bowed her head to pray, placed her cranes with a touch of elegance, bowed again, then turned on her heel and floated back to her parents. When she saw me, she pointed, spoke excitedly, then headed my way with her parents in tow. I recognized Meiko, the young student from the trolley, and rose to welcome her.

"Meiko. Good afternoon."

"Herro, Mistah Amelican," she beamed. "How you are?" Her parents stood just behind her and smiled shyly. "You have-u name-u, yes?" she asked.

"Dr. Bird. Doctor as in Professor."

"Ah, Professa Budo-san! You are *sensei, hai*?" When I nodded she clapped her hands and introduced me to her parents, the Nokamuras, who looked far too old to have a girl Meiko's age. Mrs. Nokamura wore a long, blue and white polka-dot dress, a string of pearls, and a broad-brimmed white hat that sat straight on her silver hair. Deep vertical creases scored her cheeks; her face was a tragic mask. When her gaze rested on Meiko, however, the mother's proud eyes lit up. Meiko's father wore a black suit and tie. Like Tanaka, he had blackened his hair. His sallow skin was slightly yellowed, as if jaundiced.

With painful effort we tried to visit using Meiko as an interpreter. All the while, she beamed, obviously excited to "plactise" with her rediscovered native speaker. As far as carrying on a real conversation was concerned, however, we made little progress. I cursed myself for never having bothered to learn more than a few words of polite Japanese.

Finally her father gave up on Meiko and said, "I solly bad Engrish. I speak-u heart-o. We work-u for peace. We hope-u more good-o life for Meiko."

His wife nodded and smiled, and Meiko said, "You love-a peace, *Sensei, ne*?"

I thought of the chaos, often self-imposed, that has marked my life. "Yes, Meiko. Very much."

Tears suddenly welling in her eyes, Meiko's mother spoke to her husband rapidly in Japanese. Mr. Nokamura shook his head and fluttered his hands helplessly before turning back to me to explain something very important that I could not grasp.

I shrugged. "I am so sorry, Nokamura-san. *Gomannasai, ne?*"

"*Hai, hai, gomannasai, Sensei.*"

I looked to Meiko for help. She too had become sad. "Bludda dead-o, Sensei. Long ago time."

When I just shook my head apologetically, the three of them stared at me, as if silence and their beseeching eyes could translate their pain.

A bespectacled man approached, walking slowly, with obvious effort. Around his neck the old man wore a string of jade-green cranes, and he carried a couple of thin books. It was Tanaka, looking both frail and pleased. Rather than his anonymous brown suit, he wore a long-sleeved, blue and white flowered Hawaiian shirt; sharply pressed khaki trousers; and a green-and-blue plaid tam-o'-shanter. I smiled broadly, delighted by his timing.

"Tanaka-san. Good to see you. I need your help."

Tanaka bowed to the Nokamuras, spoke a few words, and turned to me. "Ah, Mr. Bird. I am pleased be of service. You are enjoy our flower festival, yes?"

I nodded. "Please. Nokamura-san here is trying to say something from his heart. I'm just not getting it."

Nokamura spoke rapidly for a moment before the mother interrupted; tears were still welling up as she tried to smile. All the time the two were talking, Tanaka kept nodding his head, saying "*Ah so. Deseka...hai...hai!*" as if punctuating their every statement.

He turned back to me and said, "Because you are nice to daughter and because you come our Peace Park, they think you are good man." He paused and I nodded my thanks to the Nokamuras. "They want you know Meiko have brother who die of A-bomb disease many years ago, long time before Meiko is born. They pray for many, many years before the god send them Meiko. Meiko make their hearts sing. But when they think of their son, their hearts always again sad."

I thought of the encounter on the trolley and how Meiko's energy had helped brighten a very gray day. Her vitality had made even my despairing heart sing. "I am so sorry about your son," I said. "And I too am pleased that you have Meiko. She must be a delight."

Tanaka translated, nodding his head toward me once or twice, then said something that altered the mood. "*Hai!*" they said in unison when he had finished. "*Hai!*" They looked at me and smiled.

Tanaka handed the two slim books he was carrying to Meiko. Using both hands, like a Tibetan lama removing a silk *khatak,* a sacred scarf, to bestow upon a pilgrim, he removed the strand of green paper cranes from around his neck and placed it around mine. "We think is time for you make offering to Goddess of Peace and pray for all children, those lost, those living, and those not yet born to troubled world."

"But these are your cranes," I protested.

"Yes, they are mine. Every year I fold cranes to bring this place on Children's Day. My hands always hurt, so is hard to do, but when I fold paper I think of wife and daughter. I try not just think about their deaths so many, many years ago. I think also of joy we have together when daughter is born, and joy we have later, in last few months of war, after I come home from China. Heart warm again when I see families enjoy life.

"Please, Mr. Bird, accept my offering of hope for new world and good life, for Meiko and all our new children."

"Thank you, Tanaka-san. Thank you very much!" I had been on a ragged emotional edge ever since making the decision to return to Hiroshima. Tanaka's gesture fused disparate threads of hope, fear, and sadness. Unable to hold back my tears, I turned away, approached the bronze boy and girl, bowed, and placed Tanaka's gift atop the piled thousands of others. I thought of Meiko's lost brother and of Sadako, whose seemingly fruitless faith had inspired this monument and its countless pilgrims. I thought of friends who have lost children, one to sudden infant death syndrome, one to leukemia, two to suicide, and two to automobile accidents. I thought of the tens of thousands of children who died in Hiroshima and Nagasaki and of the millions of other children lost this century in seemingly endless legions of increasingly horrific wars. "Please," I prayed. "Please, Kannon. Please, Goddess of Peace."

I stared at the piled strands of cranes, then bowed and returned to my group. Looking back and forth between Mr. and

Mrs. Nokamura, I said, "I am very, very happy that you have Meiko."

Tanaka translated, obviously delighted with the little drama he had helped stage. After everyone had stood around and beamed good will at each other for a moment, he took the two slim volumes back from Meiko. Again extending his gift in both hands, he showed the books to the Nokamuras then presented them to me. "I buy these little books for you, Mr. Bird. I hope you find useful."

The parents nodded, while Meiko patted the one with a white and yellow cover. "Yes. I know. We study school-u for learn-u Engrish."

A shadow of sorrow passed over Tanaka's face as he nodded and touched the second book, *A Crane That Can Not Come Back*. "This is story of Mrs. Nanako Seto. This is journal she keep during last months of life dying in hospital. Mrs. Seto was teenager when Little Boy fall. Later she marry and have daughter. In 1957 she come down with A-bomb disease and die in 1959. Many, many others since die of A-bomb disease." He handed the book back to Meiko and added, "This is last note she make in journal. After that she is too weak. Meiko, *dozo!*" He handed her the book.

Meiko glanced over the page then shook her head. "No. Prease. This too sad-u."

Tanaka nodded, took the book back, and read, "Time to put off lights soon.... Lonely. Tears. Tears stream down... ceaselessly.... One more has died tonight. I don't want to die.

Mami, my only daughter! Nanako, Mami's only mother! Oh, this feeling.... This lonely feeling..."

We stood for a moment as if in prayer, all of us staring at Tanaka's index finger as it tapped and tapped Nanako Sado's last phrase. Tanaka then pointed to the book that Meiko had studied in her English class. "*Barefoot Gen* is about boy who lose father and many family in A-bomb fire. Gen and pregnant mother are not strong enough to free others from fallen beam, so they burn to death. Then Gen helps mother give birth to new baby."

"Please," he said, taking the book from me, flipping to the last page, and handing it to Meiko. "Please read."

Speaking slowly, Meiko read the final paragraph of Gen's story: "Every time Gen thought of the happy days which he had spent with his family, he could not help feeling lonely and sad. But he was not discouraged. He stood firmly on the ruins with his bare feet. 'I must be strong, like wheat,' he said to himself. 'I must take care of my mother and new sister as Father told me, and help to build a better world for all of us to live in.'"

Tanaka handed the books back to me. "Please, you remember, Mr. Bird. Like Gen, we must not allow selves be discourage. We know what sadness is, which maybe help us more appreciate happiness when it touch us. We live in hope—as you must. People who lose all hope just give up. They surrender and die. That is why I come Peace Park each month. That is why I fold cranes for Children's Day. And that is why you must go home and fold cranes."

Though not quite sure what I was agreeing to, or how I might proceed, I nodded and bowed. "Thank you, Tanaka-san. I will fold my cranes."

"Yes, I think so." Again he spoke in Japanese to the Noka-muras, who smiled and agreed. "Yes, Mr. Bird. We think so." He looked at his watch. "Now is time for you catch train. Good-bye."

Everything had happened too quickly. I looked at my watch and realized I would not make it back to the Peace Bell. "I don't know what to say. Thank you, Tanaka-san. I will never forget you." I turned to the Nokamuras, bowed, and smiled.

"I am so sorry, Mr. Bird. Good-bye," Tanaka urged. I turned and strode rapidly toward the Motoyasu Bridge.

"Good-bye, *Sensei*," Meiko yelled. I turned briefly, waved, and jogged toward the trolley stop. The further I jogged, the more I felt as if I were stretching some kind of spiritual umbilical cord that threatened then, and still threatens, to snap at the very next step.

❧　❧　❧

Skies remained mostly clear for the trip back to Yokohama. Comfortably alone in my seat, I spent the hours reflecting on the last few days and the creeping despair I had finally managed to stem, though not eliminate. The despair was and remains macro, in many ways abstract, impersonal, connected to the larger world. And, of course, there is much in the Hibakusha's Peace Park upon which despair can feed. For a very few moments, I allowed my mind to stand again before the dioramas of the A-bomb Museum. Like a bore tide, despair rushed back, brief but consuming.

As W. B. Yeats keened late between the two world wars:

> Things fall apart; the centre cannot hold.
> Mere anarchy is loosed upon the world,
> The blood-dimmed tide is loosed, and everywhere
> The ceremony of innocence is drowned;
> The best lack all conviction, while the worst
> Are full of passionate intensity.[31]

Technology's rampaging contributions to the "global village" ensure that we will be living much closer to each other's neighborhoods, hence more insistently in each other's face. As we are finally beginning to understand, in an age of proliferating weapons of genocide, almost any form of fear-driven fundamentalism might ignite at least regional Armageddon.

Although our era continues to confirm Yeats's deep and prophetic fears, visions antidotal to despair do exist. In my imagination, Tamiki Hara's "vision of one flower" celebrates the Hibakusha's dream of world federalism. Hara's vision pleads with us to extend our sense of family. That such extension is possible is exemplified by the century-long and tragically painful birth struggles of the European Union, where peoples with a history of war are finally practicing a more enlightened mutual self-interest.

Rather than dwelling on the darkness, however, as I had earlier in my journey, I thought mostly of the people I had met, of their hopes and fears and losses, and of their connections to the park and its themes. I thought of the three old Hibakusha on the trolley, about Meiko and her friends and parents, about the old couple I had encountered first at the Atomic Mound and later before the cenotaph. I thought of the pride and joy and hope that invigorates the Flower Festival, with its parade, floorshow, and strolling families. And I thought again of Mr. Tanaka. Through strength of spirit, love of children, and a vision of a possible future, the old soldier had somehow integrated his despair. Like the city he obviously loves, Tanaka-san is a phoenix. He helped me see the yin–yang qualities of hope and despair through a less opaque lens. Though sometimes inevitable and unconquerable, despair is a slough in which one wallows and ultimately suffocates. Hope is a beacon that, however weakly it may sometimes shine, leads us toward life. That frail beacon encourages us to act in good faith.

The sun was setting over the mountains of central Honshu, bathing the houses and terraces in the soft, warm glow of early evening. Everywhere color sparkled in the clarity of late light. I mumbled a psalm of gratitude and supplication to the gods. Hope may ultimately prove to be nothing but a thin reed in a howling wind. Yet it endures. And because it endures, hope requires us to work for peace and against nuclear proliferation, whether the proliferation be domestic or foreign. We hope and we work, as we have always known but too easily forget, for and through our children.

As this plague rages

Enraged martyrs slip between the cracks
of our once invincible moat, and torn skies
still echo the screams of the mass murdered.
At the twisted girders of once proud towers
where blind hubris reigned supreme,
our beloved cloak of innocence
lies in smoking rags around our feet.
Like the poison dust of old atomic blasts,
charred bones feed the fires of our apocalypse
and fall to earth as nameless ash.

As we pound bleak truth into our shell-
shocked minds, and strike back with engorged might,
woe to us if we forget: Fratricide
will never save the wretched of the earth.
Only open arms can heal the septic wounds
of our flailing, hate-stoked world.

Despair is a swamp where we flounder and die,
while even faint hope glimmers toward life.
In Hiroshima a grieving poet saw
"in the midst of a crumbling world
the vision of one flower." And today
In the City of Forgiveness a new phoenix shines.

LEONARD BIRD
DURANGO, COLORADO
HIROSHIMA DAY, 2004

Notes

1. "National Cancer Institute Study Estimating Thyroid Doses of I-131 Received by Americans from National Atmospheric Nuclear Bomb Tests, 1997," www.cancer.gov (accessed September 1, 2004).

2. Only after the Comprehensive Test Ban Treaty in 1992 had banned all atmospheric testing did lawsuits and public pressure begin to force the release of long-classified incriminating documents. See Carole Gallagher, *American Ground Zero: The Secret Nuclear War* (Cambridge, MA: MIT Press, 1993), xxiii–xxiv. Gallagher's large-format montage of black-and-white photographs captures the haunting faces of downwinders and atomic veterans. Each portrait is accompanied by a story. These stories shame the nation. See also Richard L. Miller, *Under the Cloud: The Decades of Nuclear Testing* (Woodlands, TX: Two-Sixty, 1991), 357–90. Miller is *the* primary source for understanding the relationship between the Nevada Test Site and the rest of America.

3. There is some argument as to "controversial." In 1953 Shot Simon, which, at forty-three kilotonnes was one of the larger detonations, attained a height of forty-four thousand feet. Because Simon was detonated only three hundred feet above ground, the blast sucked up far more particulate matter than if it had been a larger bomb detonated from, say, a balloon anchored fifteen hundred feet above the deck. Perhaps the most infamous shot was Harry (32 kilotonnes), which also climbed above forty thousand feet. Like Simon, Harry was detonated only three hundred feet from the ground and was also particularly "dirty." See Miller, *Under the Cloud*, 418–20.

4. "Current Time," *Bulletin of the Atomic Scientists* (March 25, 2003):1. See www.thebulletin.org/media/022702pr.html.

5. Mary Dickson, "Living and Dying with Fallout," *Dialogue: A Journal of Mormon Thought* 37.2 (Summer 2004):7–8. Mary Dickson is an award-winning Utah author and coproducer of the PBS documentary, *No Safe Place: Violence Against Women*. Dickson has witnessed and written extensively on downwinder issues.

6. "Current Time," 3–4.

7. John Goffman, interview with Carole Gallagher, San Francisco, March 1992, in Gallagher, *American Ground Zero*, 326–28. Goffman, the author of "Radiation and Human Health and Radiation-induced Cancer from Low-dose Exposure," is the authority on the relationship between ionizing radiation and cancer.

8. Miller, *Under the Cloud,* 462.

9. Miller, *Under the Cloud,* 210–11.

10. Dickson, "Living and Dying with Fallout," 14.

11. Ibid., 7. Dickson uses her thorough knowledge of atomic testing and downwinder issues to support her very personal and courageous story.

12. Gallagher, *American Ground Zero,* 338.

13. "Diseases Specific to Radiation-exposed Veterans," *Atomic Veterans Newsletter* 23 (Spring 2002):8.

14. R. Jeffrey Smith, "Atom Bomb Tests Leave Infamous Legacy," *Science* 218 (October 15, 1982):266–69. See also Miller, *Under the Cloud,* 373–74 and 379–83.

15. Miller, *Under the Cloud,* 444.

16. Boley Caldwell III, "NAAV Medical Data Base," *Atomic Veterans Newsletter* 17 (Spring 1995):7.

17. Tom Wicker, "Serving His Country," *New York Times,* August 29, 1993. Reprinted in the *Atomic Veterans Newsletter,* winter 1993–94, as an insert.

18. Miller, *Under the Cloud,* 384.

19. Caldwell, "NAAV Medical Data Base," 8.

20. Kildare Dobbs, "The Shatterer of Worlds," in *The Norton Reader: An Anthology of Expository Prose,* 8th ed. (New York: W. W. Norton, 1992), 427–33.

21. Yoshiteru Kosakai, *Hiroshima Peace Reader* (Hiroshima: Hiroshima Peace Foundation, 1980), 29.

22. Ibid.

23. Ibid., 29–31.

24. Ibid., 67.

25. Ibid., 45–46.

26. A large number of folding crane projects exist, many of which have Web sites. See, for example, www.sadako.org.

27. Kosakai, *Hiroshima Peace Reader,* 44.

28. Ibid., 39.

29. Fujihiko Komura, "Message in A-bomb Literature Is Irreplaceable," *Peace Culture* 1.30 (March 1993):6.

30. Ibid.

31. W. B. Yeats, "The Second Coming," in *The Collected Poems of W. B. Yeats* (New York: Macmillan, 1956), 184–85. Reprinted by permission.